THE POULTRY

Somerset-born Ruth Martin is married to an artist and has a daughter and a French son-in-law who stoutly defends British cooking – at any rate, as encountered *chez* Martin!

She has published six books on cookery and home management and also specializes in anglicizing and editing American cookbooks for the British market. She is also an interviewing journalist, feature-writer and lecturer.

This book sets out to provide the reader with a number of varied, economical and exotic ways of preparing poultry and game. So, while some of the dishes suitable for special occasions call for wine, cream or other rather expensive ingredients, there are also plenty of recipes for making family meals. For easy reference, these economical dishes have been marked with a special symbol (*E*) which appears throughout the Chicken and Turkey sections of the book. In the index they are marked with an asterisk.

Also available in Pan Books

ALL ABOUT COOKERY – Mrs Beeton
THE CORDON BLEU BOOK OF JAMS, PRESERVES
   AND PICKLES – Rosemary Hume and Muriel Downes
MISS READ'S COUNTRY COOKING
DEEP-FREEZE COOKERY – Marika Hanbury Tenison
WORLD COOKERY – Marguerite Patten
LEARNING TO COOK – Marguerite Patten
HERBS FOR HEALTH AND COOKERY – Claire
   Loewenfeld and Philippa Back
THE CONSTANCE SPRY COOKERY BOOK – Constance
   Spry and Rosemary Hume
THE MARGARET POWELL COOKERY BOOK
SPANISH COOKING AT HOME AND ON HOLIDAY –
   Maite Manjón and Catherine O'Brien
QUICK AND EASY CHINESE COOKING –
   Kenneth Lo

THE POULTRY AND GAME COOKBOOK

Compiled by RUTH MARTIN
Decorations by GILLIAN KENNY

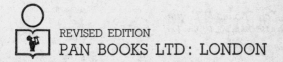

REVISED EDITION
PAN BOOKS LTD: LONDON

First published in Great Britain 1971 by
Angus and Robertson (Publishers) Pty Ltd
This revised edition published 1973 by Pan Books Ltd,
33 Tothill Street, London SW1

ISBN 0 330 23709 8

*Printed and Bound in England by
Hazell, Watson & Viney Ltd,
Aylesbury, Bucks*

CONTENTS

INTRODUCTION

The enormous growth of the poultry industry in recent times has been reflected even in the humblest kitchen. In countless homes, chicken – and even more so, turkey – once made an appearance only at Christmas-time or on very special family occasions. Now they feature frequently on the housewife's shopping list and represent good value for money. Even ducks, which were rarely seen in shops except at Christmas, are now available all the time and, since they are rather less economical, have taken over the more glamorous role that chicken once had.

The marketing of chicken halves and portions has been so hugely successful that it has now been extended to turkey, thus opening up a whole new range of possibilities for the variety-seeking cook.

However, far too many people still limit their poultry cooking to the straightforward 'roast', and it is a sad fact that the palate tires much more quickly of roast poultry than it does of roast meats. The object of this book is to show that there is an infinite variety in the ways that birds can be served – hot or cold, some very simple, others more ambitious. In addition to roasting-with-a-difference recipes, there are world-ranging ideas for using whole, half- or quarter-birds, as well as the packets of breasts and drumsticks now available. You will find too, plenty of ways to make exciting dishes out of the rather boring remains of a large cold bird.

Country-dwellers perhaps have more access to game birds than town folk, but pheasant, partridge, pigeon and so on are frequently to be found in poulterers' shops. The treatment and preparation of game birds are, therefore, included in this book, together with suggestions as to the form in which they can be brought to the table.

INTERNATIONAL CONVERSION TABLES

These conversion tables are intended to help all users of PAN cookery books – wherever they live in the world. The weights and measures used throughout this book are based on British Imperial standards. However, the following tables show you how to convert the various weights and measures simply.

International Measures

Measure	UK	Australia	New Zealand	Canada
1 pint	20 fl oz	20 fl oz	20 fl oz	20 fl oz
1 cup	10 fl oz	8 fl oz	8 fl oz	8 fl oz
1 tablespoon	$\frac{5}{8}$ fl oz	$\frac{1}{2}$ fl oz	$\frac{1}{2}$ fl oz	$\frac{1}{2}$ fl oz
1 dessertspoon	$\frac{2}{5}$ fl oz	no official measure	—	—
1 teaspoon	$\frac{1}{6}$ fl oz	$\frac{1}{8}$ fl oz	$\frac{1}{6}$ fl oz	$\frac{1}{6}$ fl oz

Conversion of fluid ounces to metric

1 fl oz	= 2·84 millilitres
35 fl oz (approx 1$\frac{3}{4}$ Imperial pints)	= 1 litre (1000 ml or 10 decilitres)
1 Imperial pint (20 fl oz)	= approx 600 ml (6 dl)
$\frac{1}{2}$ Imperial pint (10 fl oz)	= 300 ml (3 dl)
$\frac{1}{4}$ Imperial pint (5 fl oz)	= 150 ml (1$\frac{1}{2}$ dl)
4 tablespoons (2$\frac{1}{2}$ fl oz)	= 70 ml (7 centilitres)
2 tablespoons (1$\frac{1}{4}$ fl oz)	= 35 ml (3$\frac{1}{2}$ cl)
1 tablespoon ($\frac{5}{8}$ fl oz)	= 18 ml (2 cl)
1 dessertspoon ($\frac{2}{5}$ fl oz)	= 12 ml
1 teaspoon ($\frac{1}{6}$ fl oz)	= 6 ml

(All the above metric equivalents are approximate)

Conversion of solid weights to metric

2 lb 3 oz = 1 k (kilogram)
1 lb   = 453 gm (grammes)
12 oz = 339 gm
8 oz   = 225 gm
4 oz   = 113 gm
2 oz   = 56 gm
1 oz   = 28 gm

Equivalents

1 UK (old BSI standard) cup equals $1\frac{1}{4}$ cups in Commonwealth
countries
4 UK tablespoons equal 5 Commonwealth tablespoons
5 UK teaspoons equal 6 New Zealand or 6 Canadian or
8 Australian
1 UK dessertspoon equals $\frac{2}{3}$ UK tablespoon or 2 UK teaspoons

In British cookery books, a gill is usually 5 fl oz ($\frac{1}{4}$ pint), but in
a few localities in the UK it can mean 10 fl oz ($\frac{1}{2}$ pint).

Other non-standardized measures include:
Breakfast cup = approx 10 fl oz
Tea cup   = 5 fl oz
Coffee cup = 3 fl oz

Oven temperatures

Description	Electric Setting	Gas Mark
Very cool	225° F (110° C)	$\frac{1}{4}$
	250° F (130° C)	$\frac{1}{2}$
Cool	275° F (140° C)	1
	300° F (150° C)	2
Very moderate	325° F (170° C)	3
Moderate	350° F (180° C)	4
Moderately or	375° F (190° C)	5
fairly hot	400° F (200° C)	6

Hot	425° F (220° C)	7
	450° F (230° C)	8
Very hot	475° F (240° C)	9

These temperatures are only an approximate guide as all ovens vary slightly, according to the make and country of manufacture.

NOTE: The symbol (E) at the beginning of a recipe indicates that it is particularly economical.

SOUPS

HOT SOUPS

Never throw away the carcase of your poultry, particularly turkey and chicken, without extracting from it the last scrap of value and nutriment. Use the carcase to make stock from which any number of differing soups can be prepared.

BASIC CHICKEN STOCK (*E*)

1 carcase	sprigs of parsley
1 onion, coarsely chopped	sprigs of thyme
2 carrots, coarsely chopped	1 bay leaf
1 small turnip	4 pints cold water

Cut the carcase into pieces and put them into a large saucepan, add any scraps of left-over meat and stuffing. Prepare the vegetables, add the seasoning and pour on the water. In order to extract the maximum flavour, bring the pot slowly to the boil. Simmer until the liquid has reduced by about one-third (about an hour), then strain into a bowl and leave to cool.

If using a pressure cooker, take care to follow the manufacturer's instructions about over-filling. Cooking time at 15 pounds pressure is 20 minutes, and you can reduce the initial water quantity to 3 pints. When the stock is cold, remove any fat from the surface. The stock is then ready for use, but should be reboiled each day unless stored in a refrigerator. The stock should not be kept, in any case, more than three days because it encourages the development of bacteria which can lead to food poisoning.

BASIC TURKEY STOCK

Substituting your turkey carcase, follow the instructions for
Basic Chicken Stock, but increase the quantity of water by half.
These stocks can be used for any soup recipe calling for white
stock, or for any of the following.

BROWN CHICKEN SOUP (E)

1 ounce butter
carcase of bird, etc
giblets, including liver
1 or 2 small onions, sliced
1 medium tomato, cut in 4
pinch of basil

a little gravy browning
powder, or 1 oz flour and
browning drops
water
salt and pepper

Place the carcase and giblets in a large saucepan. Add the onions,
the tomato, the seasoning, any oddments of force-meat left over,
and the basil. Pour over 2 to 2½ pints of water, bring to the boil
and simmer for 2 hours. Strain into a basin. If not wanted
immediately, leave to cool, then skim off any fat. Otherwise,
keep hot.

Meanwhile, remove any scraps of flesh from bones and
carcase, chop liver and flesh very finely and add to broth. Melt
butter in a pan, mix in the gravy browning powder (or the flour
and a few drops of liquid browning). When blended and cooked,
gradually add the stock, make it piping hot and serve, garnished
with fried bread croûtons.

SERVES 4

CHICKEN AND CAULIFLOWER CREAM (E)

1 small cauliflower
1 onion, grated
2 pints chicken stock

1 level tablespoon cornflour
1 small cup milk
salt and pepper

Break the cauliflower into small pieces and mix it with the onion,
into the stock, season, bring to the boil and simmer for
30 minutes. Strain the stock into another saucepan, purée the

vegetables and blend with the stock. Mix the cornflour into the milk, stir carefully into the soup and bring back to boiling. Boil 2 minutes, check the flavour, add further seasoning if necessary. Serve with toast or fried croûtons of bread.

SERVES 4

MUSHROOM SOUP

2 oz butter	¼ pint hot milk
½ lb mushrooms, sliced	pinch of nutmeg
1 oz onion, chopped	chopped parsley
1½ oz flour	salt and pepper
1½ pints chicken stock	

Heat the butter in a pan. Add mushrooms and onion. Allow to cook for a few minutes. Sprinkle in the flour. Stir well, until flour has been absorbed. Allow to cook for a further 2 minutes. Gradually add boiling chicken stock and hot milk. Stir well. Season to taste with salt, pepper and a pinch of nutmeg. Allow to simmer for 15 minutes before serving, sprinkled with parsley.

SERVES 4

ONION SOUP AU GRATIN

4 or 5 Spanish onions, sliced or diced	toasted French bread
	grated Gruyère or Emmental
2 oz butter	cheese
2 pints stock or chicken broth	salt and pepper

Sauté onions in butter until lightly browned. Add stock or broth, either to the pan in which you have browned the onions or to a large casserole to which you transfer the onions. Salt and pepper to taste, allow the soup to come to the boil, and simmer 15 minutes.

Serve with slices of French bread heaped with the grated cheese and lightly browned under the grill. Serve with additional grated cheese.

SERVES 4

Variations

CLEAR ONION SOUP

Strain the soup. Serve with toasted French bread and grated Parmesan cheese.

ONION SOUP WITH WINE

Add ½ cup dry white wine to the broth after adding broth to the onions.

ONION SOUP IN CASSEROLE

Transfer the soup to individual heat-proof dishes. Top each one with a slice of toast and heap with grated cheese. Place in a moderate oven (375° F, Gas 5) for 10 minutes.

WATERCRESS SOUP

4 oz watercress leaves	1 level dessertspoon chopped
¼ oz butter	chervil or parsley
1 small egg yolk	1 pint chicken stock
¼ cup cream	salt and pepper

Wash and dry the watercress, chop roughly and cook it over a low flame in the melted butter for 5 minutes. Stir in the stock and seasoning and simmer for 30 minutes.
Blend the egg yolk into the cream, stir in the herb and add to the soup. Heat through but do not allow the soup to boil. Serve with bread croûtons.

SERVES 2–3

CHINESE CHICKEN SOUP

2 pints chicken broth	1 oz bamboo shoots
4 pieces dried mushrooms	salt
1 chicken breast	

Finely shred the chicken breast, bamboo shoots and mushrooms. Bring the broth to the boil, drop in the shredded ingredients, season with salt to taste. Cook gently for 3 to 5 minutes. Serve in small individual bowls.

SERVES 4

CHINESE CORN AND CHICKEN SOUP

1 large (11½ oz) tin creamed sweet-corn	3½ cups water
3 eggs	2 tablespoons cornflour
1 slice cooked ham	1 tablespoon sherry (optional)
3 cups chicken broth	2 teaspoons salt

Blend the cornflour with half a cup of the water. Put the remaining water together with the stock, salt and sherry, if used, in a large pan and bring to the boil. Add the sweet-corn, reboil and cook 4 minutes. Reduce the heat to low, dribble in the beaten eggs to form 'flowers'. Now stir in the cornflour-water mixture, stir, and continue cooking and stirring for 2 minutes after the soup has thickened. Serve with the cooked ham (chopped) for garnish.

SERVES 4-5

FRENCH GREEN PEA AND CHICKEN SOUP

3 lbs fresh peas, shelled	parsley
2 oz butter	chervil (optional)
1 onion	3 cups chicken stock
2 teaspoons sugar	¼ cup cooked white chicken meat
½ teaspoon salt	
1¼ cups water	3 egg yolks
1 young lettuce	1½ cups single cream
spinach leaves	

In a large saucepan put three-quarters of the peas, the butter, the finely minced onion, the lettuce cut in julienne strips, about 15 leaves of fresh spinach, a sprig of parsley, a few sprigs of chervil if you have it, the sugar, the salt, and water. Cover the saucepan, bring the soup to the boil, and cook it over a moderate heat until the peas are tender. Meanwhile, boil the remaining peas, in a separate pan, to add to the soup later. Strain the soup, pressing the vegetables through with the liquid or mix in a blender. Return the soup to the saucepan, add the chicken stock, stir well, and simmer over a low heat for about 15 minutes. Then add the extra peas, drained, and the chicken meat cut into very fine julienne strips. Mix the egg yolks with the cream, and add this gradually to the soup, stirring constantly. Continue cooking until the soup thickens to a creamy consistency, but do not let it boil. This makes a large quantity, sufficient for 6 to 8 servings.

TURKEY SOUP

1 turkey carcase	squeeze of orange or lemon
stock or water to cover	juice
1 onion, sliced	little sherry (optional)
bouquet garni	sprig of parsley
Worcester sauce	salt and pepper

Remove any stuffing from the carcase and reserve a little meat. Cut this into dice as a garnish. Break up bones, put into a large saucepan and cover with stock or water, allowing ½ pint for each serving. Add the onion with a little salt and pepper, bouquet garni, a dash of Worcester sauce and orange or lemon juice. Bring to the boil, then reduce heat, cover and simmer for 2 to 3 hours, skimming occasionally. Strain and allow to cool. When cold, remove all fat from surface and reheat, adding diced meat and sherry. The sherry isn't absolutely essential but it does improve the flavour.

TURKEY NOODLE SOUP

turkey carcase	bouquet garni (sprig of
1 large onion	parsley, thyme and small
4 cloves	bay leaf)
1 large carrot	2 oz noodles
2 stalks celery, with leaves	salt
6 peppercorns	

Remove any remaining meat from the carcase. Cut meat into small pieces and reserve. Crack bones and place with all remaining ingredients, except the noodles, in a large saucepan. Cover with at least 2½ pints cold water. Bring slowly to the boil. Half cover the pan and simmer very slowly for 3 to 4 hours. Strain and chill the stock. Then skim off any fat from the top. Before serving, add any reserved meat to the stock, bring it quickly to the boil and simmer for 15 minutes. Meanwhile cook the noodles until tender in a quart of boiling, salted water, then drain. Add hot, drained noodles to the soup, and serve.

SERVES 4–5

GIBLET SOUP *(E)*

1 set turkey or goose giblets	1 teaspoon salt
2 pints water	5 peppercorns
1 celery stalk	parsley (2 sprigs)
1 carrot stalk	thyme (2 sprigs)
1 onion	1 oz flour
1 clove	1 oz butter

Wash and trim the giblets, cover with the water and bring slowly to simmering. Add the vegetables, herbs, spices and seasoning and simmer for at least 2 hours. Strain. Melt the butter in a saucepan, stir in the flour and cook until it browns – take care not to burn. Gradually stir in the stock, bring back to the boil and cook, stirring, for about 5 minutes. Add the best of the giblet flesh, diced very small. Taste for seasoning and adjust as necessary. (You can make this with chicken giblets, but you will need at least 2 sets for this quantity of water, etc.)

SERVES 4

GAME SOUP

2 partridge carcases and trimmings (or equivalent in other game birds)	2 rashers lean bacon
	1 or 2 slices breast of bird
	1 celery stalk, roughly diced

1 onion, roughly diced
1 carrot, roughly diced
2 pints stock
bouquet garni of parsley,

thyme and bay leaf
½ oz butter
½ oz flour
salt and pepper

Melt the butter in a large saucepan and in it brown the carcases
and bird trimmings and fry the bacon. Remove them while you
fry the vegetables, Stir in the flour and cook till golden, then
add the stock and bring to the boil. Put back the birds and
bacon, add herbs and seasoning and simmer for about 2 hours.
Strain, add to the liquid the bird breast, diced very small, and
reheat, checking the flavour for seasoning.

CARROT AND POTATO SOUP

1½ lb potatoes, sliced or diced
1 lb carrots, sliced
1 small onion or shallot,
sliced
3 oz butter
1 teaspoon sugar

2 pints stock
a little grated nutmeg
chopped parsley
4 tablespoons thick cream
salt and pepper

Prepare the potatoes. Melt half the butter in a saucepan, add
the onion, and cook until softened but not brown. Add potatoes
and carrots, stir well, add sugar and a little salt. When the
vegetables have absorbed the butter, add the stock and cook
until vegetables are tender. Rub through a sieve or put into a
liquidizer. Return to the saucepan. Reheat, adjust the seasoning, add a dash of nutmeg and a little more stock if soup is too
thick. Just before serving, add remaining butter and cream, and
stir in a little freshly chopped parsley.

SERVES 4–5

PARMENTIER SOUP

1 lb potatoes, thickly sliced
2 or 3 leeks (white part only)
2 oz butter
2 pints stock
4 tablespoons milk

3 tablespoons cream
chopped parsley, chives or
chervil
salt and pepper

Prepare the potatoes. Clean the leeks, cut into pieces and sauté in half the butter, taking care not to brown them. Add potatoes, stock, and salt. Cook until the vegetables are soft. Rub through a sieve, or put into a liquidizer. Return to the saucepan, adjust the seasoning, and reheat. Just before serving, stir in the rest of the butter, milk and cream. Sprinkle with freshly chopped parsley, and serve hot or cold.

SERVES 4

POTATO AND WATERCRESS SOUP (E)

1 lb potatoes
1 large onion, sliced
1 bunch watercress, chopped
1½ pints stock

¼ pint milk
a little grated nutmeg
salt and pepper

Peel the potatoes and cook with the onion in the stock until tender. Rub through a sieve, or put into a liquidizer. Return to the saucepan, add the milk, and reheat. Adjust the seasoning, add a dash of grated nutmeg and, before serving, stir in the chopped watercress.

SERVES 4

POTATO AND CELERY SOUP (E)

1 lb potatoes, quartered
½ head celery
2 onions, sliced
1 oz butter
1½ pints stock

¼ pint milk
chopped parsley
grated Cheddar cheese if liked
salt and pepper

Separate the sticks of celery, wash thoroughly and cut into pieces. Prepare the potatoes and onions. Melt the butter in a saucepan, add the celery and onion, and cook gently without browning. Add the potatoes, stock, and seasoning. Bring to the boil, and simmer gently until the vegetables are cooked. Rub through a sieve, or put into a liquidizer. Add the milk, reheat, and adjust the seasoning. Serve piping hot, sprinkle with freshly chopped parsley or grated cheese.

SERVES 4–5

COLD SOUPS

Cold soup on a hot day is as appetizing as a hot soup is on a cold day. All of the last three soups mentioned above are delicious and refreshing when served iced in summer weather. Another favourite summer soup is Vichysoisse, although this can be served hot if preferred.

VICHYSOISSE (E)

1 oz butter
2 leeks, finely chopped
½ onion, finely chopped
1 stalk celery, chopped
1 potato, sliced
2 tablespoons top of milk

1 pint chicken stock
Worcester sauce
pinch nutmeg
chopped chives
salt and pepper

Melt the butter, add the leeks and onion. Cook slowly until transparent, then add celery, potato, salt, pepper and stock. Cook until all vegetables are tender, add other seasonings to taste. Put through a sieve, and add the milk (also more stock if needed to make up quantity to 1½ pints). Serve chilled, with sprinkling of chopped chives.

SERVES 3–4

ICED CUCUMBER SOUP (*E*)

1 large cucumber	1 oz butter or good quality
1 large onion, thinly sliced	margarine
1 pint stock	1 lemon
½ pint milk	salt and pepper

Fry the onion in the fat till tender. Add the stock and the cucumber, partially peeled and cut into small chunks. Season to taste, and simmer for 25 minutes. Remove from heat, pass the mixture through a sieve and allow to cool. Then add the milk, and chill the soup in the refrigerator. Serve in cold soup bowls topped with thin lemon slices.

SERVES 3–4

SOUP FROM WHOLE BIRDS

For a first-class Chicken Broth or for the famous Cock-a-Leekie, you need a whole small boiling fowl.

CHICKEN BROTH (*E*)

1 small boiling fowl	2 teaspoons salt
4 pints water	¼ teaspoon pepper
1 carrot	2 celery stalks or a bunch of
1 onion	herbs (thyme, parsley,
1 bay leaf	marjoram)
1 blade mace	1 tablespoon Patna rice
piece of lemon rind	1 tablespoon chopped parsley

Wash and joint the bird, put in a large pan with the water and giblets, seasoning and vegetables, bring slowly to the boil and simmer for 3 to 4 hours, adding more water if needed. Strain the broth through a colander, return it to the pan, skimming off as much fat as possible with a metal spoon. Sprinkle in the rice, bring back to the boil and simmer for 20 minutes. Serve, sprinkled with the chopped parsley.

The chicken meat may be served as a separate dish, or used for a fricassée or other recipe requiring chicken flesh. You may, of course, chop some of the meat finely and add it to the broth.

Variation

TO MAKE A THICK CHICKEN SOUP (*E*)

2 pints chicken broth (as above)	1 oz flour
4 oz cooked chicken	4 tablespoons milk
1 oz butter	a little nutmeg

Blend the chicken meat in an electric blender or pass through a sieve. Melt the butter, stir in the flour, add stock slowly, heat till boiling. Cook for 2 minutes, then gradually add puréed chicken meat. Add salt and pepper if required and a dash of nutmeg. Finally add the milk, reheat but do not allow to boil.

COCK-A-LEEKIE (*E*)

1 small boiling fowl	water to cover
4 oz prunes	2 teaspoons salt
1 lb leeks	pepper

Soak the prunes overnight. Clean the fowl, wash the giblets, place in a large saucepan and cover with water. Bring slowly to simmering point, add salt and pepper, and simmer for 1 hour. Then add the leeks, cleaned and sliced, and simmer for a further 2 hours. Finally add the prunes, stoned and halved, and simmer again for 30 minutes. Serve the chicken meat in the soup or as a main course.

BELGIAN CHICKEN SOUP

Although called a soup, this is a really substantial dish. The
addition of wine gives a luxury touch which justifies your
serving it on special occasions.

1 chicken	½ oz butter
2 carrots, sliced	parsley, thyme and a bay leaf
3 leeks, finely shredded	½ bottle dry white wine
4 sticks celery, finely shredded	1 pint chicken stock
2 onions, finely shredded	salt and pepper
1 lemon	

Cook the carrots gently in the butter. Rub the chicken all over
with the lemon, and place in a deep saucepan or a large casserole.
Pour over it the chicken stock, then add the vegetables, herbs
and seasoning. Bring to the boil. Next, add the wine. Cover
closely, bring up to boiling point again, then reduce the heat
immediately and simmer on a low flame or in a slow oven until
the bird is tender. This will depend on the age and size of the
bird, but the use of a roasting bird is preferable.

When ready, take out the chicken and carve it. Lay in a deep
serving dish, pour the stock over the carved bird and garnish
with the vegetables, a little finely chopped parsley, and some
croûtons of fried bread.

ADDITIONS TO SOUPS

As you can see, the preceding soups made from whole birds can
form substantial one-dish meals of liquid and solids. Served
with crusty bread, they are very satisfying repasts. Some of the
earlier soup recipes in this section, such as Turkey Noodle Soup,

Chinese Corn and Chicken Soup and the French Green Pea and Chicken Soup make a meal in themselves for lunch or supper. But any liquid soup can be given extra bulk by the addition of noodles, spaghetti or other pasta, or easily-made dumplings.

SEMOLINA DUMPLINGS (*E*)

2 eggs
½ oz butter
½ pint milk

4 oz semolina
salt and pepper

Heat the milk and butter together, gradually stir in the semolina, bring to the boil and cook, stirring, for 5 minutes. Season, and take off the stove. Separate the eggs, beat the yolks briefly and stir into the semolina. Fold the stiffly-whipped whites into the mixture. Have ready a pan of boiling salted water over a low heat, and drop in the mixture a teaspoonful at a time. In about 7 or 8 minutes the dumplings will rise to the top, indicating that they are cooked. Drain and add to your prepared soup.

CHICKEN LIVER DUMPLINGS

4 chicken livers (uncooked)
2 oz butter
2 oz flour
1 slice bread

1 tablespoon freshly
chopped parsley
1 egg
milk
salt and pepper

Chop the livers very finely and mix with the flour, butter (softened), herbs, seasoning and egg. Soak the bread in milk, and add as much of it as is needed to bind the mixture. Beat together very thoroughly, form into small balls, and set aside for about 1 hour. Simmer the dumplings in the soup for 10 to 15 minutes.

POTATO DUMPLINGS (*E*)

1 lb potatoes   1 small onion, grated
1 egg   (optional)
4 oz self-raising flour   salt and pepper
1 tablespoon chopped parsley

Peel the potatoes thinly, and boil in salted water. Drain well,
and put through a 'ricer' or sieve, or mash well. Add the egg,
flour, parsley, seasoning, and onion if liked. Mix well together,
and form into small balls, using a little flour to prevent sticking.
Set aside for about 1 hour. Place the dumplings in the soup
and simmer until the dumplings are cooked, 15 to 30 minutes
according to size.

CHICKEN

In this section you will find information on the preparation and cooking of chickens, fresh or frozen, whole or jointed. First, however, here are some general principles to help you in choosing your bird.

SIZES AND TYPES

Poussins   Smallest and youngest birds on the market, weighing up to about 1½ pounds and serving one or two people. They are best split down the middle, brushed with melted butter and grilled 10 to 15 minutes per side.

Spring chickens Birds of 2 to 3 pounds serving two to three people.

Chickens   Birds of 3 to 5 pounds serving up to five people.

Capons   Desexed birds of 6 to 8 pounds serving seven or eight people (see Jointing, p. 34).

Boiling fowl   Older birds, not suitable for roasting but admirable for boiling or cooking by other slow-heat methods or for use in soup making.

FRESH BIRDS

Most housewives today buy oven ready birds, but if you have occasion to buy one which is unplucked, or alternatively, plucked but not drawn, here are some points to note.

Feathers should be soft and full, wing quills should come out easily, comb and wattles should be small and there should not be any long hairs.

The skin of a young bird should be white and unwrinkled, the breastbone pliable and the breast plump. The stiffer the breast-bone and the harder and dryer the feet, the older the bird. Beware of shrunken eyes, soft, flabby feet, or greenish tinge of flesh. Never buy a bird with a 'gamey' smell.

FROZEN BIRDS

Only first-quality birds are processed by the manufacturers, so you have no worries on that score. However, it is of the greatest importance that the bird should be *thoroughly thawed* before cooking. This applies equally to chicken joints and all other frozen poultry.

The time required to thaw a whole chicken from solid, at room temperature, is 8 to 15 hours, depending on size. Bacteria are killed during the cooking process. However, if the bird is incompletely thawed and is then cooked only for the time allowed for wholly soft birds, parts of the meat will be under-cooked with consequent risk to the consumer.

DRESSING AND PREPARATION

In these days of 'oven-ready' poultry, the housewife is not often called upon to practise the arts of plucking, drawing and dressing birds. However, since no poultry and game book would be complete without instructions on these points, they are included here for the benefit of those who may have their own birds, or may be given unprepared birds or, indeed, may wish to buy them in this form from butcher or poulterer.

PLUCKING AND SINGEING

Plucking can be a tedious job unless it is done immediately after the bird is killed and while the body is still warm. Place the bird breast downwards on a large sheet of paper or clean cloth, draw out one wing and commence to pluck the underwing feathers, taking only a very few at a time, so as not to tear the skin. Work towards the breast, then down to the tail, and repeat on the other side. The large flight feathers at the end of the wings will need hard pulling or they can be snapped away from the direction of growth.

Once all the feathers have been removed, some hairs or down may remain and this can be singed away with a lighted taper. Do not, however, singe off any stray feathers because these will give off a strong, unpleasant smell which will permeate the flesh of the bird and spoil it.

If you happen to have the unenviable task of plucking a cold bird, tie its feet together with string and hang over a hook fixed firmly to the wall, then proceed as above.

One time-honoured method of making plucking easier is to plunge the bird very briefly in almost-boiling water. But once the feathers have been removed, make sure that the bird is thoroughly dry before using the lighted taper on hairs and down.

DRAWING

Cut off the head from about two inches down the neck. Turning the bird on to its breast, insert a sharp knife under the skin of the neck and slit it down to the base. Loosen the skin, then cut off the neck at the trunk. Throw away the head, but keep the neck to add to the giblets for stock-making. Slit the skin down just enough to allow you to insert your fingers to loosen the crop and gizzard.

Slip a sharp knife under the leg skin just above the foot, bend and snap the bone, then draw out the tendons, one at a time, by inserting a skewer under them, and, holding firmly on to the foot, drawing them from the flesh. This is a necessary operation, because these tendons, if left in, will make the flesh tough. Detach the feet which can, if you wish, be added to the stock ingredients.

Cut a slit at the vent end of the bird but take care not to pierce the gall bladder and other entrails, as this would give a bitter flavour to the flesh. Insert your fore- and middle fingers and gently loosen the heart and other organs and gradually draw them out. Draw down the crop and gizzard from the neck end. With a clean cloth wrapped round your index finger, take out the lungs by pressing along the ribs, starting at the backbone. When the bird is clean, trim the vent neatly.

Carefully separate the liver from the gall bladder, reserve the neck, gizzard (cleaned of its grit container), liver, heart and —if liked—the feet for making stock, and burn or otherwise dispose of the inedible remains; that is, the head, intestines, lungs, crop and grit from the gizzard.

WIPING OR WASHING
Fresh (non-frozen) birds
It has long been considered that wiping out the cavity with a clean, damp cloth is all that is necessary, and that rinsing the bird through with water destroys a certain amount of its flavour. Some people, however, feel impelled to wash the bird, so in the final analysis this must be a personal choice.

Frozen birds
It is of the utmost importance that frozen birds are thoroughly thawed before cooking (see page 31). Thereafter the situation regarding washing or wiping is the same as for fresh birds.

STUFFING (see page 36) for suggested stuffings, also individual recipes)

The clean bird may now be stuffed at the neck end and the skin folded over and stitched with needle and cotton to keep it in place. This stitching should, of course, be cut away when the bird is dished up after cooking.

If the bird is large, a different stuffing can also be placed in the body cavity, but the quantity should be limited so that there is plenty of room for the hot air to circulate in the bird during cooking.

Alternatively, stuffing can be baked separately, in a dish, or made into small balls, brushed with oil or melted fat, and cooked for 15 to 25 minutes, depending on the heat of the oven.

TRUSSING

Trussing is done purely for the sake of neat appearance and easier carving. It makes no other difference to the final cooked result.

Laying the bird on its back, fold the wing tips back towards the backbone and press the legs well into the side to raise the breast. Thread a trussing needle with clean, fine string and pass the needle through the first wing joint, through the bird and out through the wing joint on the other side. Insert again in the first wing joint, pass again through the body to the first wing joint on the other side. Tie the ends with a bow for easy removal after cooking.

Make a slit in the skin above the vent and push the 'parson's nose' through the slit. The legs may simply be tied firmly to the 'parson's nose,' or another piece of string may first be run through the hock joints and body (twice) under the breast-bone and tied with a bow.

JOINTING

The simplest way of preparing a dish using chicken joints is, of course, to buy the pieces ready cut. If you want to serve more numerous but somewhat smaller pieces, buy generously-sized portions and redivide them at the bone joints, so that you can obtain two servings from each leg joint. You can, of course, also buy packets of drum-sticks and packets of chicken breasts for particular dishes.

TO JOINT A WHOLE BIRD

Lift the legs, one by one, from the body, cut through the skin and press the leg outwards till the joint breaks away from the back-bone. If the bird is small, use whole. Otherwise, redivide at the knuckles with kitchen scissors. Turn the neck of the carcase towards you, cut off the pinions (cook these with the giblets to make gravy) and cut the breast meat straight along the breast-bone to the wing joint. Break the joint and cut it away so that with the breast meat, it is in one piece. Again, this can be redivided to make two portions.

Cut down the back of the carcase from vent to neck end, to provide two more portions.

With a large chicken, it is possible to divide into nine portions, as follows.

legs   – 2 portions each   – 4 portions
wings – 1 portion each   – 2 portions
breast – removed whole by cutting through ribs
              with scissors and divided lengthwise   – 2 portions
back   – divided lengthwise   – 1 portion

Appetites vary as much as bird-sizes, so this is merely a guide to the number of portions obtainable. Whether you serve one or more such portions depends upon circumstances.

COOKING THE BIRD

Larding or barding

To overcome the tendency of poultry flesh to dryness, the breast can be either larded or barded. Larding is done by threading a special larding needle with long thin strips of hard fat bacon and threading it through the flesh, leaving the ends protruding.

Barding is covering the breast with rashers of very fat bacon and, if necessary, tying them in place.

Cooking times

Heat the oven at 425° F (Gas 7) and cook the bird at this temperature for the first 20 minutes. Then lower to 375° F (Gas 5) and allow 20 minutes for each pound of oven-ready weight, plus the original 20 minutes. Baste every 20 to 30 minutes and uncover the breast for the final 15 minutes, to brown.

STUFFINGS FOR ROAST CHICKEN

While it is not, of course, absolutely necessary to stuff a chicken, this has long since been a traditional way of serving poultry.

You can, if preferred, simply put a sprig of rosemary in the cavity to impart a delicate flavour. But the use of different stuffings at different times will give more variety to your own menu and, since the stuffings themselves are in the main not expensive to make, they have a distinct economy value in making the chicken meat go further.

See also Stuffing (page 34).

FORCEMEAT (*E*)

4 oz white bread-crumbs
1 oz suet
2 teaspoons parsley
¼ teaspoon grated lemon rind

1 rasher streaky bacon
1 egg
pinch dried thyme
salt and pepper

Chop the parsley finely, chop or shred the suet, and chop the bacon. Mix the dry ingredients with a fork, then bind with the egg, previously well beaten. Do not pack the mixture too tightly into the bird but allow room for swelling during cooking and thus prevent the stuffing from becoming too stodgy.

HERB AND RELISH STUFFING (*E*)

4 oz white bread-crumbs
2 teaspoons mixed dried herbs (parsley, thyme, chives, marjoram)
1 small onion

2 teaspoons cranberry and orange relish or cranberry sauce
orange juice (if necessary)
1 egg
salt and pepper

Chop the onion finely and put in a basin, together with the breadcrumbs, herbs and cranberry relish. Mix well, season to taste with salt and pepper, then bind with the egg, previously beaten, and add a little orange juice if necessary.

This stuffing is equally suitable for duck or turkey, but in the latter case you would need to increase the quantities by using either half as much again of each ingredient, or double.

VEAL AND CHESTNUT STUFFING

6 oz pie veal	marjoram
3 oz chestnuts	1 egg
1 teaspoon oregano or	salt and pepper

Cook, peel and skin the chestnuts and mince them together with the pie veal. Season well. Add the herb and bind with the egg, well beaten. Bake 30 minutes if cooked separately.

CELERY AND PARSLEY STUFFING (*E*)

4 oz white bread-crumbs	¼ teaspoon grated lemon rind
4 oz celery, chopped	1 rasher streaky bacon
1 oz butter	1 egg
pinch thyme	salt and pepper
2 teaspoons chopped parsley	

Chop the bacon, mix together in a basin with the bread-crumbs, thyme, parsley and seasonings. Cook the celery gently in the melted butter for about five minutes, then add all to the crumb mixture. Stir in the lemon rind, then bind the mixture with the egg, previously beaten.

LIVER STUFFING

liver from the chicken	1 oz suet, chopped or
2 oz calves' or lambs' liver	shredded
4 oz white bread-crumbs	½ teaspoon lemon juice
1 rasher streaky bacon	(optional)

1 egg

½ teaspoon dried thyme

1 medium onion

¼ teaspoon chopped garlic

1 teaspoon chopped parsley

salt and pepper

Boil the onion until soft. Then chop it finely, add to the livers, also chopped. Mix with the crumbs, suet, and other dry ingredients. Season to taste, add the lemon juice, if used, then bind the mixture with the egg, previously well beaten.

MUSHROOM STUFFING (E)

4 oz bread-crumbs

2 teaspoons chopped parsley

1 oz butter

¼ teaspoon dried thyme

2 rashers streaky bacon

1 egg

2 oz mushrooms

salt and pepper

½ teaspoon lemon juice

Chop the bacon and mix together in a basin with the bread-crumbs, herbs and seasoning. Melt the butter in a pan and in it cook the mushrooms very gently. Do not let them brown. When just cooked, drain and chop, and add to the dry ingredients in the basin. Pour the remaining melted butter into the mixture, add the lemon juice, season, and bind the mixture with the egg, previously beaten.

PINEAPPLE AND RICE STUFFING

4 oz rice

½ teaspoon salt

1 small (7½ oz) tin pineapple pieces

a little black pepper

1 teaspoon dried sweet basil

1 onion, chopped

1 egg

Cook the rice in two cups water in a covered saucepan for about 15 minutes. Drain and rinse with fresh water. Drain well and add the salt and pepper. Chop the pineapple into small pieces, and place in a bowl with the rice and onion. Mix in the herbs. Bind with beaten egg.

RAISIN AND RICE STUFFING

2 oz raisins, ready-stoned or seedless	1½ tablespoons chopped parsley
2 oz almonds	1 oz melted butter
2 oz rice, cooked	1 egg
1 onion	salt and pepper

Blanch and chop the almonds, mix into the cooked rice and the raisins. Chop the onion finely, add to the mixture. Season with salt and pepper. Add the parsley, pour over the melted butter, mix well and finally bind with the well-beaten egg.

TANGERINE AND MUSHROOM STUFFING

1 tangerine	2 oz mushrooms, chopped
4 oz rice	1 tablespoon fresh chopped parsley
½ teaspoon salt	beaten egg
1 onion, chopped	
2 celery sticks	

Cook and season the rice as for Pineapple and Rice Stuffing above. Fry the onion and mushrooms lightly in a little oil, then add to the cooked rice. Mix in the chopped parsley and the celery sticks, finely chopped. Peel the tangerine, remove the pips, then cut the peel into thin julienne strips and the flesh into smallest possible pieces, and add to the rest of the mixture, combining very thoroughly. Bind with beaten egg.

PRUNE AND WALNUT STUFFING

3 oz soft bread-crumbs	½ oz butter
1 small onion, grated	1 teaspoon dried thyme
3 oz prunes, stoned and chopped	1 egg
2 tablespoons chopped walnuts	salt and pepper

Mix the bread-crumbs with the onion, prunes and walnuts, then add the butter, cut into small pieces. Beat the egg, and with it bind the mixture into a handleable consistency, adding a little milk if necessary.

HOT WHOLE CHICKEN DISHES

Here are some ideas for getting away from the conventional stuffed, roast chicken yet still serving a whole bird. Chicken Maryland, Chicken Braised in Wine, Coq au Vin and Chicken Normandy are eminently suitable for dinner guests, but don't take a chance with Pernod Chicken unless you are sure they like aniseed flavour!

CHICKEN LIMOUSIN

1 chicken (about 4 lb)	4 oz sausage meat
2 dozen chestnuts	4 mushrooms (fairly large),
cooking oil	minced
chicken stock	1 teaspoon parsley, minced
1 celery stalk	1 onion, chopped
$\frac{1}{2}$ teaspoon sugar	salt and pepper
3 oz butter	

Cross-cut the chestnut shells on the flat side and heat them in a little oil in a heavy frying-pan until the shells begin to open. Peel the chestnuts and place them in a pan with the celery stalk, sugar, $\frac{1}{4}$ oz of the butter, a pinch of salt and enough chicken stock just to cover. Simmer for about 20 minutes.

Meanwhile sauté the onion in 1 oz of the butter until soft and transparent. Then mix this with the sausage meat, the mushrooms, the parsley and a little seasoning. Stuff the chicken with this mixture, then brown the bird all over in the remaining butter melted in a heavy casserole.

Place the casserole in the oven at 350° F (Gas 4) and cook uncovered for 20 minutes. Drain the chestnuts and reserve their stock. Place the chestnuts around the chicken, add half cup of the strained chestnut stock and continue to cook the chicken, still uncovered, for about an hour or until it is brown and tender. Add more stock during cooking time if it becomes necessary so that the dish will not dry out. You should have at the finish a reduced but adequate amount of sauce to serve with the bird.

SERVES 3–4

WHOLE ROAST CHICKEN MARYLAND

A recipe for Chicken Maryland, using chicken joints, is to be found on page 57. Below, however, is a slightly varied version of that dish using a whole chicken and one or two other ingredients to add variety. This is a very colourful dish to serve garnished as suggested for the family or a special meal.

1 roasting chicken (about	chicken)
4 lb)	1 level teaspoon curry powder
2 oz butter	3 bananas
¼ pint stock (preferably	salt and pepper

Fritters

½ tin sweetcorn kernels	2 tablespoons milk
(11½ oz size)	frying oil or fat
1 egg	salt and pepper
3 oz self-raising flour	

Garnish

3 large tomatoes	a little butter
½ tin sweetcorn kernels	salt and pepper

Sprinkle the chicken with salt, pepper and the curry powder. Place in a roasting tin and dot with butter. Pour the stock around the bird. Cook at 400° F (Gas 6) for 1¼ to 1½ hours, basting the bird once after it has been cooking for about 15 minutes.

For the fritters, mix half the sweetcorn kernels with the egg, flour and milk into a batter, and season. Heat a little oil in a frying-pan and drop the batter in spoonfuls into the hot fat. Fry the underside until golden, then turn and fry on the other side. Lift out of the pan, drain on absorbent kitchen paper for a few moments before arranging them on a dish.

About 15 minutes before the chicken is ready for serving, skin the bananas, split them in half lengthways, and place them round the chicken. Halve the tomatoes, scoop out the centres, sprinkle with salt and pepper and fill with sweetcorn kernels. Dot with butter and place in the oven with the chicken, for about 10 minutes. To serve, arrange the chicken on a hot dish with the bananas and some of the stuffed tomatoes around it. Serve the rest with the fritters. Serve gravy separately.

SERVES 4–5

BRAISED CHICKEN AMBASSADOR

1 chicken (about 3 lb)	2 oz mushroom stalks,
8 oz pork sausage meat	chopped
1 oz butter	1 level tablespoon plain flour
¼ pint white wine or dry cider	salt and pepper
2 oz onion, chopped	

Stuff the crop end of the chicken with the sausage meat, then retruss the bird. Melt the fat in a frying pan and quickly brown the chicken on all sides. Remove from the fat and place in a casserole just a little larger than the chicken. In the same fat, fry the onion until just tender, then the mushroom stalks. Add the white wine (or cider) and pour this sauce over the chicken. Cover closely and cook in a fairly hot oven 400° F (Gas 6) for 1 hour, or longer, depending on size (see p. 35).

To serve, remove the chicken from the casserole, place on a flat serving dish and keep hot. Strain the stock into a saucepan and add the flour blended with a little cold water. Bring to the boil, stirring all the time and simmer gently for 5 minutes. Season to taste. Serve separately or poured over the chicken. If liked, the dish can be garnished with buttered button onions and mushrooms.

SERVES 3–4

CHICKEN BRAISED IN WINE

1 chicken (about 4 lb)	1 bouquet garni
2 oz butter	$\frac{1}{2}$ pint dry, white wine
2 tablespoons olive oil	$\frac{1}{4}$ pint chicken stock
4 oz fat bacon, diced	a little cognac
4 oz carrots	salt and pepper
4 shallots	

Heat the butter and oil in heavy, flameproof cocotte or casserole just large enough to hold the chicken. Dice the bacon pieces and sauté in the fat until golden. Remove the bacon; add the coarsely-chopped shallots and carrots and cook, stirring constantly, until the vegetables soften, then add the chicken and brown on all sides. Return the bacon bits to the pan, pour over the heated cognac and flame. Add bouquet garni, salt and freshly-ground black pepper to taste, dry white wine and chicken stock. Cover the bird with a piece of buttered paper, cut to fit the casserole, with a small hole in the centre to allow steam to escape. Cover the casserole and simmer gently over a very low heat until tender ($1\frac{1}{2}$ to 2 hours). Add more wine or a little chicken stock during the cooking if the sauce reduces too quickly.

SERVES 3–4

ROAST CHICKEN WITH BUTTER AND LEMON (*E*)

1 chicken	$\frac{1}{2}$ to 1 teaspoon dried tarragon
1 lemon, cut in half	(depending on its strength)
2 oz butter	salt and pepper

Wipe the chicken thoroughly. Rub it all over first with the lemon and then with butter, placing ½ oz fat inside the cavity, together with the lemon halves and most of the tarragon. Season with plenty of salt and pepper and a little tarragon. Place the bird breast side up in a baking dish, put it in a medium oven (350° F, Gas 4) and baste every 15 minutes for about 1 hour. The skin should be crisp and golden, and the chicken should be quite moist, with a very tangy flavour.

SERVES 4

PERNOD CHICKEN WITH FENNEL

Pernod is a favourite French drink with a unique flavour. The following recipe recommends 3 tablespoons of Pernod to be used in the closing stages of cooking, but if you are in doubt about this quantity it is suggested that you reduce this to 1½ tablespoons in the first place and if you find that you would like a stronger flavour you can use the full amount on another occasion.

1 chicken (2½ to 3 lb)	1 glass dry white wine
2 oz butter	½ teaspoon dried fennel
4 teaspoons olive oil	1 head celery, diced
2 petite Suisse cheeses	6 leeks, diced
3 tablespoons Pernod	salt and pepper

Mash the petites Suisses and add salt, pepper and fennel. Stuff the chicken breast with this mixture. Grease a large ovenware dish, place the chicken in it and roast in the oven at 350° F (Gas 4) for 20 minutes. When browned, add the wine and the oil. Spread out the vegetables in the dish and season. Cook in the oven at 325° F (Gas 3) for 1 hour. Add Pernod 10 minutes before serving. Serve the chicken surrounded by the vegetables.

SERVES 2–3

POACHED SPRING CHICKEN WITH EGG SAUCE

1 chicken (about 3 lb)	4 tablespoons dry white wine
1 small onion stuck with	or cider
4 cloves	2 egg yolks
sprig of basil	1 oz butter
sprig of parsley	1 hard-boiled egg
sprig of tarragon	1 teaspoon chopped parsley
1 blade of mace	salt and pepper
¼ pint chicken stock	

Garnish

1 hard-boiled egg   chopped parsley

Put the onion stuck with cloves, the herbs and mace inside the carcase of the chicken, with a sprinkling of salt and pepper. Heat the stock and wine in a thick stewpan. Put the bird in, cover the pan closely and poach slowly for about 45 minutes, or until tender. Take out the bird, remove the skin and flavourings and keep warm. Thicken the liquor with egg yolks, at the same time adding the butter in small knobs. Add chopped hard-boiled egg and parsley, and season to taste. Pour over the bird and garnish with sieved hard-boiled egg and chopped parsley.

SERVES 2–3

FRENCH POACHED CHICKEN

1 chicken, young and plump	1 oz butter
(about 3 lb trussed)	

Court-bouillon

4 pints chicken stock	2 slices lean bacon
2 carrots, diced	pinch of thyme
2 small turnips, quartered	1 bay leaf
2 celery stalks, diced	2 sprigs parsley
4 leeks, chopped	truffles (optional)

Make the court-bouillon by heating the chicken stock and in it placing the carrots, turnips, the celery stalks, and the leeks

(with most of their green tops removed), the bacon and herbs.
Simmer for 10 minutes and then put in the chicken and bring
to simmering point. The original recipe calls for a number of
slices of truffle inserted under the skin of the breast and leg
of the bird and if you can do this, so much the better, of course.

Simmer, covered, for 30 minutes after the stock comes back
to the boil. Then turn off the heat and let the chicken stand and
continue to poach in the hot stock for 20 minutes. Remove the
chicken to a hot dish, pour over it a little of the stock so that it
will not dry out, and keep it warm. By now the vegetables should
be tender. If they are not, continue to cook them while you
make the sauce. In a small saucepan reduce 1¼ cups of the stock
to ½ cup over a high flame. Taste it for seasoning and then take
off the heat and whip in the butter previously creamed. Serve
the chicken surrounded by the vegetables and hand the sauce
separately.

SERVES 2–3

COQ AU VIN

Coq au Vin is a famous dish, but as with many classics, recipes
do vary in certain respects. On page 59 you will find a Coq au
Vin recipe using a bird cut into 6 pieces. The following recipe
however allows for the chicken to be cooked whole. Another
variation is that in this case the brandy is flamed and in the
recipe on page 59 the brandy is added to the sauce.

1 chicken (2 to 3 lb)	20 shallots
lemon juice	8 oz mushrooms
5 oz butter	2 garlic cloves
1 small wine-glass brandy	1 dessertspoon plain flour
1 bottle red wine	salt and pepper

Season the chicken well with salt, pepper, garlic and lemon
juice. Melt 3 ounces of the butter in a heavy-based saucepan
and in it brown the chicken all over. Heat the brandy in a ladle,
set it alight and pour it over the chicken. Move the saucepan
about until the flame has died down, then add the wine and the
chicken giblets. Cover with a tight-fitting lid and simmer gently

for about 1½ hours. Meanwhile brown the shallots in an ounce of the butter. Add them immediately to the chicken together with the mushrooms.

When the cooking time is up, first remove the giblets, then lift the chicken, carve it and arrange the pieces on a hot dish. Beat the remaining butter into the flour and divide it into tiny balls. Drop these into the sauce and bring it slowly to just below boiling point. Stir until the sauce has thickened and pour it over the chicken pieces and arrange the shallots and mushrooms over the top. You can if you wish serve small crescents of fried bread around the edge of the dish.

SERVES 2–3

CHICKEN NORMANDY

Although this is nicer when made with the ingredients listed below, a more economical but perfectly acceptable version (*E*) can be made by omitting the Calvados or brandy and using 2 tablespoons cider vinegar topped up with chicken stock to make a quarter pint.

1 boiling fowl (about 6 lb)	¼ pint cider
3 cooking apples, cored and quartered	1 teaspoon Calvados or brandy
4 oz streaky bacon	2 egg yolks
3 small onions	salt and pepper
1 oz butter	

Place the apples inside the prepared bird. Chop half the bacon and fry gently till the fat is extracted. Add the butter, melt, and then brown the chicken carefully in this fat. Transfer to a deep fireproof dish. Chop the onions finely, add to the dish, with salt and pepper. Cover the bird with the remaining bacon, cut into strips, pour the cider round, cover closely and cook slowly (300° F Gas 2) for about 3 hours. When the chicken is cooked, drain off all the liquor into a saucepan. Beat in the egg yolks, stir over a very low heat until the mixture thickens, add the Calvados or brandy, then pour over the chicken and serve immediately.

SERVES 5–6

TOP-OF-STOVE CHICKEN (*E*)

Here is a whole chicken recipe which you can use even if you only have a gas-ring in your bed-sitter. It is easy and economical, and the bird does not shrink as much as in roast chicken.

2 oz bacon fat, dripping or cooking oil	1 stick celery, chopped
1 chicken (2 to 2½ lb)	1 teaspoon salt
sprinkling mixed spice	1 small cup stock (or ½ cup water, ½ cup wine)
1 large onion, chopped	
flour	2 teaspoons cornflour
2 large carrots	2 oz mushrooms
1 leek, chopped	tomato purée
	salt and pepper

Melt the fat or oil in a large, heavy saucepan. Meanwhile rub the chicken well with flour, sprinkle with salt, pepper and spice. Rub well in, then brown the chicken, breast downwards, in the hot fat. Meanwhile prepare the onion, carrots, leek and celery. Put the onion in to brown with the chicken. When the breast is well browned, turn the bird the right-side up, add all the vegetables, the salt, the stock or wine and water mixture. Cover with a really tight-fitting lid, turn down the heat, and leave the chicken to simmer till almost cooked (about 1½–2 hours). Blend 1 cup of the pot liquor with the cornflour and a dessertspoon of tomato purée. Return it to the pot, stir till it thickens, add the mushrooms and cook a further 15 minutes uncovered.

SERVES 2–3

HOT DISHES USING CHICKEN JOINTS

CHICKEN JOINTS

In many of the following recipes you are given the alternative of starting with a whole bird or with chicken joints.

Now that chicken is so conveniently packaged, you can buy whatever parts of the bird seem best suited to the dish you want to prepare, or to the particular tastes of your family. Some people prefer to eat chicken legs, others think the wing and breast meat is more delicate.

Sometimes it is more economical to buy a whole bird and joint it yourself. This way, of course, you get the giblets for making stock and flavouring a stuffing. But if you want to serve smaller chicken portions, you can buy somewhat larger quarter-chickens and divide each into half, as follows.

Leg quarter	Using a sharp knife and a cutting board, cut across the joint where the drumstick joins the thigh.
Wing quarter	Stand the quarter, breast uppermost, on your cutting board. Then with your sharp knife, cut downwards. This ensures that you will leave some breast meat on the wing.
Drumstick and breast	These, too, can be bought in separate packages, which is both more convenient and more economical than starting with a whole bird when using recipes intended for these cuts. This is specially important in the case of chicken breasts, and you will find the recipes which use them grouped together on pages 72 to 78.

Whatever you use, whether it is a whole bird or portions, make sure that the meat is thoroughly thawed out before you begin cooking.

FRIED CHICKEN (E)

Nothing could be simpler and more straightforward than plain fried chicken. Simply flour the quarters, either whole or divided into two portions, as explained above, and place into two inches of hot fat in a saucepan or sauté pan. When the pieces are brown, turn them and continue cooking over a lower heat, with the pan uncovered. Whole quarters will take 25 to 35 minutes to cook, according to size.

P.G.C.—3

SOUTHERN FRIED CHICKEN (*E*)

For this variation, flour the quarters or joints, then dip them first in beaten egg and then in bread-crumbs. Fry briskly in two inches of hot fat until crisp, then more gently until tender, taking care not to overcrowd the pan. For a crisp finish, cook the chicken with the lid on for the first ten minutes, then take off the lid and complete the cooking over a moderate heat.

SOUTHERN FRIED CHICKEN WITH SAVOURY RICE (*E*)

4 chicken portions or a 2 to
2½ lb chicken, jointed
2 oz plain flour
2 oz butter
1 level teacup long grain rice
1 large onion, chopped

2½ cups stock or water (a
stock cube may be used)
1 level teaspoon salt
2 rounded tablespoons grated
Parmesan cheese
salt and pepper

Season the flour with salt and pepper and coat the chicken portions. Melt the butter in a frying-pan and brown the chicken on the fleshy side for about 10 to 15 minutes. Transfer to an ovenproof dish or plate and cook a further 20 minutes at 400° F (Gas 6). While the chicken is cooking in the oven, add the onion together with the rice, to the butter remaining in the frying-pan. Cook over a moderate heat for 5 to 10 minutes or until the rice takes on a golden colour. Add extra butter if necessary. Stir in the stock and salt (if unseasoned stock or water is used), continue cooking over a very low heat until all the liquid is absorbed (about 20 to 25 minutes), stirring occasionally. At the end of the cooking stir in the cheese, heating only long enough to melt the cheese. Pile the rice on a large, flat dish, arrange the chicken pieces on top and garnish with parsley.

SERVES 4

SPANISH CHICKEN WITH SAFFRON RICE

Spanish chicken

4 chicken portions or a 2 to
2½ lb chicken cut into joints
2 oz butter
2 oz streaky bacon
1 clove garlic, finely chopped
1 medium onion, finely sliced
4 oz mushrooms, sliced
2 tomatoes, cut in small

wedges
1 small red pepper, chopped
1½ oz plain flour
¾ pint stock, or stock and
milk mixed
3 tablespoons single cream
3 tablespoons sherry
salt and pepper

Saffron rice

1 level teacup long grain rice
generous pinch of powdered
saffron

1 level teaspoon salt
nut of butter
2½ cups of boiling water

Brown the chicken portions on the fleshy side in the butter in a frying-pan. Transfer the chicken to a casserole. Lightly sauté the bacon, garlic, onion and mushrooms in the fat remaining in the pan, then spread over top of chicken. Arrange tomato wedges over top of the mixture, then sprinkle the red pepper on top. Add an extra ½ ounce of butter to the pan, then stir in the flour and cook over a moderate heat for 1 to 2 minutes. Add the stock and bring to the boil, stirring constantly. Finally, stir in the cream and the sherry and seasoning to taste. Pour over the ingredients in the casserole, cover and cook approximately 1¼ hours at 350° F (Gas 4).

About half an hour before serving time, stir the rice, salt and saffron into the boiling water in a saucepan. Cover and cook gently over a very low heat until all the water is absorbed (20 to 25 minutes). Stir in the butter and turn into a serving dish. Serve with the Spanish chicken.

SERVES 4

CATALONIAN CHICKEN

1 chicken (2½ to 3 lb) or 4
large joints, each cut in two

1 oz butter
1 tablespoon oil

12 button onions
1 oz flour
½ pint giblet stock
4 tablespoons white wine
1 dessertspoon tomato purée

½ lb chestnuts
½ lb sausages
fried croûtons to garnish
salt and pepper

Remove the giblets from the chicken and simmer in a little water to make stock. Cut the chicken into eight joints. Heat the butter and oil in a large pan and fry the joints and onions until golden brown all over. Remove from the pan and arrange in a casserole. Add the flour to the pan, stir in the stock, wine, purée and seasoning and bring to the boil, stirring. Pour the sauce over the chicken, cover and cook in a moderate oven, 375° F (Gas 5) for 30 minutes.

Meanwhile slit the chestnuts, cover with water, bring to the boil and simmer gently for 10 minutes; drain and peel. Fry the sausages until brown. Add the chestnuts and sausages to the casserole and cook for a further 15 minutes. Arrange the chicken and sausages in a warm serving dish, spoon the sauce over and garnish with the croûtons.

SERVES 4–6

GRILLED OR BARBECUED CHICKEN HALVES (E)

4 small chicken halves
½ teaspoon lemon juice
olive oil or melted butter

1 teaspoon crushed coriander
salt and pepper (preferably
freshly ground)

Wipe the chicken thoroughly. Sprinkle the lemon juice over the halves and brush them with olive oil or melted butter. Rub all over with the coriander, salt and pepper. Grill (or barbecue over medium hot coals) for 35 to 40 minutes, turning from time to time so that the chicken cooks evenly.

SERVES 4

GRILLED CHICKEN, AMERICAN STYLE

1 chicken (about 2 lb) or	½ level teaspoon salt
4 ready-cut joints	1½ level teaspoons dried
1 tablespoon lemon juice	marjoram (optional)
2 cloves garlic, crushed	8 large mushrooms, roughly
3 oz butter or margarine	chopped
pinch of nutmeg	parsley to garnish

Cut the chicken into four joints and rub them with lemon juice. Place the garlic in the grill pan without the rack, add 2 oz of the butter and heat until melted. Turn the joints in the butter and grill under medium heat for approximately 20 minutes, turning and basting frequently. Shortly before cooking is finished, melt the remaining butter in a frying pan, add the nutmeg, salt and marjoram, then the mushrooms and cook gently for 5 minutes. Arrange the chicken on a flat dish with the juices poured over. Garnish with the mushrooms and a sprinkling of chopped parsley.

SERVES 4

BACON DRUMSTICKS (E)

A simple dish which is ready in 30 minutes, during which time you can cook your accompanying vegetables on top of the stove. The quantities given make three servings, but with simple arithmetic you can expand or contract this recipe to fit your requirements.

6 chicken drumsticks	12 oz streaky bacon

Remove the rind from the bacon and, starting at the thick end, wind the bacon round the drumsticks. Pack into a casserole and cook at 400° F (Gas 6) for 30 minutes, uncovered. The bacon does the job of basting for you.

SERVES 3

CHICKEN CHORON

4 chicken joints or 1 whole chicken, jointed

For the sauce

1 teaspoon shallot, finely chopped	3 oz butter
4 tablespoons dry white wine	1 teaspoon tomato purée
2 egg yolks	few drops lemon juice
grated rind and juice of 1 small orange	2 tablespoons cream (optional)
	salt and pepper

Grill the chicken pieces, as in recipe on p. 53 but omit the garlic. When they are almost ready, start making the sauce. This should be served immediately it is cooked, but you can if you wish stir in two tablespoons of cream to prevent it from separating if you need to keep it warm for a few moments. Put the shallots and the wine in a small saucepan and cook until the liquid is reduced to about 2 dessertspoons. Strain it into a bowl, add the egg yolks, grated rind and juice of the orange and the tomato pureé. Place the bowl over a saucepan of boiling water, add the butter, a teaspoon at a time and whisk in each piece before adding the next. If there is any sign of the mixture 'scrambling' take the bowl from the saucepan and drop in a teaspoon of cold water. Continue the cooking, adding cold water again if necessary, and when all the butter is used season with salt and pepper and then add a few drops of lemon juice. Pour over the grilled chicken and serve as quickly as possible.

SERVES 4

CHICKEN WITH ORANGE AND ALMOND SAUCE

4 chicken quarters	1 level dessertspoon caster sugar
salt, pepper and paprika	1½ oz blanched almonds, shredded and browned
2 oz margarine	
3 oranges	

Sprinkle the chicken quarters with the seasonings. Heat the margarine in a large pan and fry the chicken until golden brown all over. Cover the pan, reduce the heat and cook gently for

30 minutes or until the joints are tender. Meanwhile, squeeze the juice from two of the oranges, remove the skin and pith from the third and cut into segments. Remove the chicken quarters from the pan and arrange on a hot serving dish. Drain the excess margarine from the pan and add the orange juice, segments and sugar to the pan. Bring slowly to the boil, stirring, and allow to boil rapidly for 2 to 3 minutes. Adjust the seasoning, pour the sauce over the chicken, sprinkle with the almonds and serve.

SERVES 4

CHICKENBERRY CASSEROLE

2 tablespoons corn oil
1 roasting chicken (about
3 lb) cut in quarters, or
4 ready-cut large chicken
joints
½ clove garlic, finely chopped
(optional)

4 level tablespoons jellied
cranberry sauce
1 pint water
1 large packet tomato soup
2 tablespoons white wine
4 oz mushrooms, peeled and
sliced

Heat the corn oil in a deep pan and add the chicken and the garlic (if used). Brown the chicken quickly on both sides. Remove the chicken from the pan. Rub the jellied cranberries through a sieve and add to the saucepan with water and contents of the packet of tomato soup. Bring to the boil, stirring. Stir in the wine and replace the chicken. Cover and cook gently for 30 minutes. Add the mushrooms and continue cooking for a further 15 minutes. Place the chicken on a serving dish and pour the sauce over.

SERVES 4

BAKED SUSSEX CHICKEN (E)

4 chicken portions
salt
3 oz butter

1 clove garlic, crushed
(optional)
2 packets potato crisps
1 oz grated Cheddar cheese

Preheat oven to 350° F (Gas 4). Sprinkle the chicken joints with salt. Melt the butter in a saucepan with the crushed garlic, if used. Crush the potato crisps with a rolling pin, then mix them with the cheese. Dip the chicken pieces in the melted butter, then coat each piece evenly with the crushed crisps and cheese mixture. Arrange the chicken in a single uncrowded layer in a shallow baking tin. Remove the garlic from any remaining butter and trickle the butter over the pieces. Bake, uncovered, on the middle shelf for approximately 40 minutes. This is delicious served hot accompanied by a crisp, green salad.

SERVES 4

CHICKEN MARENGO

1 roasting chicken (2 to 2½ lb)
1 lemon
4 oz mushrooms
1 clove garlic, finely chopped
½ cup brown stock
1 tablespoon tomato purée

3 tablespoons olive oil
1 large wine-glass white wine, Madeira or sherry
salt and cayenne pepper
parsley and thyme

Joint the bird neatly and brown the pieces in the hot olive oil for about 10 minutes. Remove, and prepare the sauce by stirring in the tomato purée, stock, garlic, sprig each of parsley and thyme, wine, salt and pepper. Replace the chicken, cover and cook on a low heat for 45 minutes. Next, add the mushrooms, and juice of half a lemon. Cook for a further 20 minutes. Remove herbs and serve in a deep dish garnished with fried bread croûtons, sprigs of watercress and thin halved lemon slices.

SERVES 4

NORMANDY CHICKEN (CASSEROLED VERSION) (E)

4 chicken joints
1½ oz butter
1 medium onion, or several small ones, sliced
2 to 3 cooking apples

2 rashers bacon
¼ pint cider
thyme, parsley, bay leaf
salt and pepper

Melt the butter in a pan, brown the chicken joints all over, then take out and place in a casserole. Fry the onion gently for 5 minutes, then add the bacon, cut finely, and the apples, previously peeled, cored and rough-cut. Cook till the mixture turns colour, then transfer to the casserole, with the chicken joints. Season well, pour in the cider, adding a little water if necessary. Add a sprig of thyme, two sprays of parsley and half a bay leaf. Cover closely. Cook for 1 to 1½ hours at 300° F (Gas 2).

This recipe assumes the use of a whole bird, jointed. For a smaller quantity, purchase half a bird or individual joints and reduce other ingredients accordingly.

CHICKEN MARYLAND

1 young chicken	butter, margarine or bacon
little flour	dripping
1 egg	salt and pepper
bread-crumbs	

Garnishes

1 medium banana per person

Corn fritters

4 oz flour	1 egg
1 cup sweetcorn (either	½ cup milk
frozen, or scraped from	cooking oil or fat
cobs)	salt and pepper
1 teaspoon baking powder	

Joint the bird into 8 portions and roll in the flour seasoned with salt and pepper. Coat with egg and bread-crumbs, and fry gently for about 20 to 25 minutes in fat not less than ¾ inch deep. When tender and golden brown, lift and drain well. Serve with the bananas, sliced lengthways and fried in butter or margarine and accompanied by corn fritters, made as follows.

Mix flour, salt and baking powder together. Beat the egg, add a dash of pepper and a little milk. Make a well in the flour and pour in the egg mixture, beating gradually and forming a batter. Add milk for correct batter consistency, then stir in the sweetcorn. Drop tablespoonfuls of the mixture into a little hot fat or oil. Cook till golden brown on both sides. Drain well before serving.

SERVES 4

WEST INDIAN CHICKEN

1 young chicken (about 2 lb)	1 teaspoon curry powder
2 onions, sliced	small bunch mixed herbs
4 oz butter	(thyme, parsley, tarragon,
2 green peppers, sliced	1 bay leaf)
1 tablespoon flour	pinch of saffron strands
3 tablespoons dessicated	salt, pepper, and a good
coconut	pinch of cayenne
½ pint boiling water	

Joint the chicken, and season with the salt, pepper and cayenne. Melt half the butter in a deep pan, and in it brown the chicken pieces. In another pan in the remaining butter, fry the onions and peppers. When they, too, are lightly browned, sprinkle the chicken joints with flour, add the onions, peppers and butter, and cook gently, allowing the flour to brown, too.

Make, meanwhile, some coconut milk by pouring the half-pint of boiling water on to the dessicated coconut, allow to stand for 15 to 20 minutes, then squeeze liquid through muslin. Pour the coconut milk into the pan, add the herb bouquet, the curry powder, and the saffron already soaked in a little hot water. Mix well, cover closely, and allow to simmer gently for about 45 minutes. To serve, place pieces on a dish, pour the sauce over them, serve with plain rice, boiled and well dried.

SERVES 4

CHICKEN WITH SWEET-CORN (*E*)

4 chicken joints	1 (11½ oz) tin sweetcorn
2 oz mushrooms, sliced	¼ pint chicken stock
1½ oz butter	salt and pepper
1 medium onion, chopped	

Melt the butter in a pan, brown the chicken portions all over and transfer to a warm casserole. Season with the salt and pepper. Cook the mushrooms and onion together in the pan. Then add the chicken stock, mix, and pour over the chicken pieces. Spoon the sweetcorn around the chicken, cover, and cook for about 45 minutes at 375° F (Gas 5).

SERVES 4

COQ AU VIN

1 cockerel or chicken (2½ to 3 lb)	1 to 2 cloves garlic, crushed
4 rashers bacon	bunch of mixed herbs
4 oz spring onions	½ bottle Burgundy or other good red wine
4 to 6 oz mushrooms	½ pint (approx.) stock or water
4 oz butter	glass of brandy
2 tablespoons flour	salt and pepper

Melt about 3 ounces of the butter in a deep pan. Dice the bacon and fry it, together with spring onions, till they are golden brown. Cut the bird into pieces (not more than 6), rub each with flour. Add to pan, sprinkle with a little flour, and allow to brown. Next, add the mushrooms and continue cooking for a few moments. Pour in the wine a little at a time, then add the stock or water, already heated. The pieces should now be just covered with liquid. Add the garlic, the bunch of herbs, and pepper and salt to taste. Cover with liquid, and allow to simmer for about 30 to 45 minutes or until the bird is cooked. Meanwhile mince the liver.

When ready, lift out the meat and arrange in a serving dish. Remove the bunch of herbs, strain the liquid, and transfer the onions and mushrooms to the dish. Make a roux with the remaining butter and 1 tablespoon flour, then remove from heat and add the minced liver. Stir well and, finally, add the brandy. Reheat, but do not let the sauce boil again. Pour the sauce over the bird and serve.

SERVES 4

Variations

While a young cockerel or, if unobtainable, a chicken, is preferable for this dish, an older bird or a boiling fowl may be used. In that case, extend the simmering time accordingly.

The brandy can be omitted altogether, or can be added to the pan before the wine and stock, and flamed. If you have been able to reserve the blood of the bird, this should be added with the liver and brandy.

CHICKEN MORNAY

4 joints of roasting chicken
bread-crumbs
2 oz butter
2 oz flour
½ cup chicken stock

½ cup milk or cream
2 tablespoons grated
Parmesan cheese
salt and pepper

Make a roux by melting the butter and blending in the flour. Cook gently for 5 minutes, taking care not to let the mixture turn brown. Then add the stock gradually, stirring all the time. Season to taste. Cook a further 3 minutes, then draw from flame and gradually add the milk or cream. Return to a very low heat, cook again for 2 or 3 minutes, then stir in the grated cheese. Dip the chicken joints in this sauce, then roll them in bread-crumbs until thoroughly coated. Fry the pieces in butter or margarine until tender. Serve with French fried potatoes and lettuce hearts tossed in French dressing.

SERVES 4

HUNGARIAN PAPRIKA CHICKEN

1 chicken (2½ to 3 lb) or
4 chicken joints
1 medium onion, finely
chopped
1 green pepper, sliced
4 tomatoes (ripe), quartered
1 heaped tablespoon
Hungarian paprika

1 teaspoon plain flour
¼ pint stock
3 oz pork dripping
5 oz sour cream (or fresh
cream soured with juice of
half a lemon)
salt and white pepper

Melt the pork dripping in a large, heavy pan, and in it fry the onion, until transparent. Take the pan off the heat and stir in the paprika. If using a whole chicken, cut into four and add this together with the giblets to the pan (otherwise use your chicken joints). Add the pepper and tomatoes with the stock and bring to the boil. Simmer for about 45 minutes or until the chicken is tender, seasoning with a teaspoon of salt. Remove the chicken pieces from the pan and keep hot. Add to the sauce a half teaspoon white pepper and the cream and flour mixed together. Cook gently for about 5 minutes, then sieve finely. Reheat the sauce and pour over the chicken pieces.

SERVES 4

INDIAN CHICKEN CASSEROLE

1 chicken (about 2 lb) or	1 clove garlic
4 chicken joints	1 cardamom
1½ level teaspoons powdered	½ level tablespoon cumin
ginger	1 level tablespoon coriander
1 level teaspoon salt	¼ pint yoghurt
2 lb onions	½ pint water
2½ oz butter or ghee (see note)	5 peppercorns
1 level tablespoon turmeric	

Skin the chicken or chicken joints. Prick all over with a fine skewer, rub in the ginger and the salt and leave for 30 minutes. Chop half the onions and fry in the ghee or butter until evenly brown. Stir into the onion the clove of garlic, already crushed, then lift the onion from the pan and drain. Take the seeds from the cardamom and cook them in the fat briefly, then add the chicken together with the turmeric, cumin, coriander, and yoghurt and cook until the yoghurt is almost dry. Pulp the cooked onion, add the water and pour this mixture over the chicken joints. Thinly slice the remaining onions. Put them on top of the chicken mixture together with the peppercorns and transfer the whole dish to the oven, tightly covered. Cook at 325° F (Gas 3) for about one hour. An enamelled iron casserole is ideal for cooking this dish. If you have no suitable receptacle to use both on top and inside the stove, start the dish in a frying-pan and transfer to a casserole at the point where the pulped onion is to be poured over the chicken pieces.

Note Ghee is clarified butter and is used in Indian cooking in preference to any other kind of fat. To make ghee, melt butter in a pan over a low heat. When it comes to the boil, sprinkle with a little cold water, to check the froth. When the sizzling ceases, throw in a sprig of mint and a bay leaf. Heat for a few moments longer, then strain. When cool enough pour into a jar and keep, covered, in the refrigerator.

SERVES 4

INDIAN CHICKEN PILAU

1 chicken (about 2 to 2½ lb)	4 cloves
6 oz butter	4 or 5 peppercorns
2 onions, thinly sliced	3 or 4 cardamoms
2 cloves garlic, crushed into	1 small teaspoon salt
a cup of water	pinch of saffron
12 oz rice	3 eggs
½ pint yoghurt	water or chicken stock
1 teaspoon cinnamon	

Hard-boil the eggs, and reserve for garnish. Parboil the rice, and reserve. Joint the chicken neatly. Melt the butter in a strong saucepan. When hot, add the onions and cook till golden brown. Remove onion rings and reserve. Now put the chicken joints into the butter and brown lightly all over. Add the salt, peppercorns, cloves, cinnamon and garlic. Then add the yoghurt, together with sufficient water or chicken stock to simmer the chicken. Allow to cook gently for about 15 minutes, then add the rice, sprinkle with the cardamom seeds and cover very closely. Simmer for about 30 minutes, or until rice and chicken are cooked, add the saffron soaked in a tablespoon of boiling water. Remove to serving dish, and garnish with onion rings and slices of hard-boiled egg.

SERVES 4

HOT DISHES USING CHICKEN JOINTS   63

PORTUGUESE CHICKEN (*E*)

A simple, tasty meal using ingredients you are almost certain
to have in stock.

4 chicken joints	1 onion, thinly sliced
3 tomatoes, peeled and sliced	1½ oz grated cheese
2 oz butter	salt and pepper

Melt the butter in a warm casserole. Brush it over the chicken
portions, season with pepper and salt and arrange in the
casserole. Arrange the tomatoes and onion on top of the chicken
pieces. Sprinkle with the grated cheese, cover and cook at
375° F (Gas 5) for 40 minutes. Remove the cover and return
to the oven for a further 10 minutes or so, to brown.

SPANISH PAELLA

Half a chicken	1 or 2 cloves garlic, crushed
chicken bouillon cube	saffron strands (or powder)
12 oz rice	6 to 8 black olives
3 tomatoes, sliced	olive oil
2 onions, sliced	1¼ to 1½ pints hot water
2 peppers (red or green),	shellfish (see below)
sliced	salt and pepper
1 small (5 oz) tin peas	

Paella ingredients can be varied according to pocket and
inclination, but ideally it should contain several varieties of
shellfish – shrimps, prawns, cockles, mussels, crab or lobster
meat, oysters – about 2 cupfuls in all. The olives are optional;
the peas can be fresh, frozen or tinned; a small quantity of
chopped bacon may also be added, and so can one or two
Spanish spiced sausages (*chorizos*). Runner beans, coarsely
chopped, can be substituted for peas, or a mixture of both may
be used. Paella should be cooked in a large flat pan and served
direct from it. If nothing suitable for table use is available, cook
in a heavy frying-pan and transfer to a preheated serving dish.

Cut the chicken into 3 neat portions. Make a chicken stock
with the hot water and soup cube. In a little of the liquid soak

2 saffron stalks (or a good pinch of powdered saffron) ready for use later. Pour about ¼ inch of olive oil into the bottom of the pan. Add the garlic (1 or 2 cloves, according to preference) together with the onions and sauté for a few moments. Add the chicken pieces, brown lightly on both sides, then add the olives, the tomatoes and the peppers. If using runner beans or fresh peas, put them in at this stage. Then add the rice, stirring to prevent burning, till the rice changes colour. Pour in the stock gradually, allowing the rice to absorb the moisture. Add the saffron soaked in stock, salt and pepper to taste, and simmer the mixture over a low heat, stirring from time to time. When the rice is almost cooked, add the shellfish and the tinned or frozen peas (thawing them first). Continue cooking till rice is cooked, then transfer to serving dish if necessary. Garnish with a few shrimps and peas, and bring to the table piping hot.

Note If bacon or *chorizos* are used, they should be added at the same time as the chicken.

SERVES 3–4

BENGAL CURRY

1 small chicken or 4 chicken joints
1 clove garlic, finely chopped
3 oz butter or ghee
2 onions, chopped
¾ pint stock
salt

1 level tablespoon curry powder
2 level tablespoons tomato purée
small quantity milk
a few almonds
1 small apple

Melt the butter and in it brown the onions and garlic. Add the apple, chopped and unpeeled. Divide the chicken quarters in half and add to the pan. Next put in the almonds, curry powder, purée, seasoning, 1 tablespoon milk, stock, and simmer gently uncovered until the chicken is tender and cooked. The liquid will reduce to a thick gravy. Serve on boiled long grain rice, together with chutney, peas and chopped hard-boiled eggs.

SERVES 4

VIENNESE CHICKEN

1 small chicken or 4 chicken joints	1 tablespoon tomato purée
2 onions, chopped	$\frac{1}{4}$ pint stock
3 rashers bacon, chopped	$\frac{1}{4}$ pint sweet vintage cider
1 oz butter	2 tablespoons cornflour
1 teaspoon paprika	1 clove garlic, crushed
	salt and pepper

Melt the butter in a large pan, brown the chicken joints then add the onion, bacon, and garlic. Cook gently for 10 minutes, then add the tomato purée, stock, cider, salt and pepper. The chicken joints should just be covered. Place the lid on the pan and cook very slowly for 1 to 1$\frac{1}{2}$ hours. When ready to serve, lift the chicken pieces from the sauce and place on a serving dish. Blend the cornflour with 2 tablespoons cold water and stir into the sauce in the pan. Bring it to the boil, stirring constantly. Cook for 2 minutes after the sauce has thickened, then pour the sauce over the chicken pieces.

SERVES 4

CHICKEN LORRAINE (*E*)

6 oz shortcrust pastry	evaporated milk
$\frac{1}{2}$ chicken or 2 joints	4 oz coarsely grated cheese
1 cup water or stock	1 egg
1 large onion	bread-crumbs
1 small (6 oz) tin unsweetened	salt and pepper

Wash and cut the chicken joints, place in a saucepan with the onion, sliced, and the water or stock. Cover and simmer until tender. Leave to cool in the stock. Meanwhile, roll out your ready-prepared pastry and line a flan case about 8 to 9 inches in diameter. Bake blind as for Chicken and Celery Flan, page 92.

Make the cheese sauce by bringing the evaporated milk to the boil, then turning down the heat to simmering point. Add the cheese, season with salt and pepper and simmer until the cheese melts. Use the chicken stock to thin this sauce. Take all the chicken flesh off the bones, chop roughly and add to the sauce. Beat the egg thoroughly and add to the chicken mixture.

Pile into the flan case, top with bread-crumbs and bake for ten minutes in a moderate oven.

You may prepare this flan well in advance, but if you are cooking it from cold, then allow a little longer for it to heat through in the oven.

SERVES 4–6

AMERICAN SMOTHERED CHICKEN

1 chicken or 4 joints
1 heaped teaspoon paprika
3 oz butter or chicken fat

¾ cup dry vermouth
¾ cup cream
a little milk

Cut the chicken into 8 pieces and shake them in a paper bag with a mixture of pepper, salt and flour. Make sure that every piece is well coated. Brown the chicken in the butter or fat and arrange in a large casserole. Sprinkle generously with paprika, then pour over the vermouth, cream, the juices of the frying-pan, and enough milk almost to cover the chicken. Bake uncovered at 375° F (Gas 5). Turn the chicken pieces occasionally and stir the sauce which should be thick and curd-like. Cook until the chicken is very tender and almost leaving the bones, then serve on rice, either plain boiled, or boiled then fried in butter with a little onion and a pinch of herbs.

SERVES 4

FRENCH SPRING CHICKEN PIQUANTE

half a spring chicken (*poussin*)
per person
1 tablespoon Worcester sauce
1 tablespoon tomato purée
1 teaspoon grated onion
1 clove garlic
bay leaf

pinch of basil
3 oz butter
4 tablespoons vinegar
3 tablespoons red wine
½ teaspoon paprika
salt and pepper

Wash, dry and brush each half bird with melted butter. Melt 2 ounces of the butter in a saucepan, blend into it the tomato

purée, the Worcester sauce, the onion, garlic and basil. Add the
bay leaf and cook gently for two or three minutes. Then, add
the vinegar, salt and pepper to taste, the paprika and, lastly,
the wine. Simmer for a further 3 to 4 minutes. Place the halved
birds on a grill rack greased with the remaining butter and cook
briskly until golden. Then reduce the heat and continue cooking.
Baste continuously with the sauce. When the birds are quite
cooked, strain the sauce, pour over and serve immediately.

GERMAN CHICKEN IN BEER

4 chicken joints	salt
8 oz German pork sausage	freshly ground black pepper
2 large onions, sliced	1 oz lard
a little flour	1 pint light ale

Skin and cut the sausage into 4 pieces. Mix the salt and pepper
into the flour and toss the chicken pieces in the mixture. Melt
the lard in a pan, brown the chicken joints all over, transfer them
to a casserole. Fry the onions in the remaining fat, adding a
little extra if required. When the onions are golden brown, add
to the casserole, put in the sausage pieces and pour over the
casserole any remaining fat in the pan. Pour half the ale into
the frying-pan, bring slowly to the boil, and stir and scrape
round the pan to incorporate any small pieces which remain.
Allow the beer to boil for 2 minutes, then pour over the ingredients of the casserole together with the rest of the pint of ale.
Cover and cook in a slow oven 300° F (Gas 2) for about 1½ hours.
Finally, raise the heat high and cook for a further 10 minutes
uncovered.

SERVES 4

SWEET AND SOUR CHICKEN (E)

Although this recipe is very good with new potatoes, you can
omit potatoes altogether from the casserole and serve with
jacket, baked or sautéed potatoes. The tangy, delicious flavour
makes this a very acceptable – and economical – dinner dish for
guests who appreciate something a little different.

4 chicken joints
1 lb small new potatoes
2 oz flour or cornflour
1 small (6 oz) tin concentrated frozen orange juice, or the juice of 2 large oranges
1 tablespoon wine vinegar
1 tablespoon brown sugar
1 teaspoon ground ginger
1 large orange
½ pint chicken stock

Season the flour or cornflour and shake the chicken joints in it. Fry the pieces until golden brown on either side and place in a casserole. Mix together the orange juice, vinegar, sugar, ginger and stock. Pour over the chicken, cover and cook for 45 minutes at 350° F (Gas 4). Next, add the potatoes and cook for a further 30 minutes. Meanwhile remove the rind and pith from the orange, cut the rind into thin strips and the flesh into slices. Place on top of the chicken and cook the dish for a final 15 minutes.

SERVES 4

HOT CHICKEN BAKE (*E*)

2 oz margarine
1 jointed chicken
8 oz skinless pork sausages
4 rashers bacon
2 tomatoes, skinned and
sliced
1 medium onion, finely chopped
chopped parsley
salt and pepper

Melt the fat in a small baking tin. Lay in the jointed chicken, cut side uppermost, baste and cook in a hot oven, uncovered, for 10 minutes (425° F, Gas 7). Meanwhile cut the sausages into ¼ inch rounds, mix with the chopped bacon, the tomatoes, onion and the seasoning. Remove the chicken from the oven, baste, and turn the pieces. Lay the savoury sausage mixture on the top and return the dish to the oven for a further 20 to 25 minutes, or until the chicken is tender. Serve garnished with chopped parsley.

SERVES 4–6

CHICKEN IN ROKA DRESSING (*E*)

1 chicken (or 4 joints)	1 bottle Roka Blue Cheese
2 to 3 tablespoons seasoned	Dressing
flour	paprika

Wipe, trim and joint the chicken. Coat each piece in the seasoned flour. Dip the floured joints in the dressing until evenly covered and place in a casserole. Sprinkle the paprika lightly over the chicken, cover and place in a moderate oven 350° F (Gas 4) for 50 to 60 minutes. Remove the lid of the casserole for the last 10 to 15 minutes of cooking time to allow for browning.

SERVES 4

CHICKEN DIANE

4 chicken joints	1 little minced garlic or garlic
8 oz pork sausage meat	salt
1 tablespoon chopped parsley	1 tomato, chopped
1 small onion, finely chopped	1 green pepper, finely chopped
pinch paprika	a little stock
	salt and pepper

Brown the chicken joints in butter. Meanwhile mix together in a bowl the sausage meat, parsley, onion, paprika, pepper, garlic or garlic salt, tomato and green pepper. Season with salt and pepper to taste, and bind with a little stock or hot water. Grease four pieces of kitchen foil and place a portion of this mixture on each. Place a browned chicken quarter on top, sprinkle with salt, pepper and paprika and fold over to make a neat, airtight parcel of each chicken piece. Bake in a preheated oven at 350° F (Gas 4) for 50 minutes. Allow a little longer if the chicken quarters are particularly large. Serve with baked jacket potatoes cut open with a pat of butter inserted in each.

SERVES 4

ANNIVERSARY CHICKEN

4 chicken quarters or
8 drumsticks
4 rashers streaky bacon
4 oz mushrooms (button
mushrooms preferably)
2 small onions, finely chopped

2 large cups inexpensive red
wine
2 teaspoons chopped parsley
flour
salt and pepper

Wash and dry the chicken pieces. Dredge with flour and brown them all over in a little butter melted in a large, heavy pan. At the same time fry the onion in this fat. Chop the bacon finely, add it to the pan and turn the heat down to simmering point. Add the parsley, seasoning and wine and simmer uncovered until the liquid has reduced to about half. Now put in the mushrooms (whole if small, otherwise sliced), and continue cooking until the chicken is tender. This will take from 25 to 35 minutes according to the size of the joints.

SERVES 4

TOMATO CHICKEN CASSEROLE

4 chicken portions
4 small onions, chopped
4 rashers streaky bacon
8 oz tomatoes, skinned and
sliced
1 teaspoon brown sugar

1 teaspoon vinegar
2 tablespoons oil or 2 oz
margarine for frying
1 dessertspoon tomato purée
salt and pepper

Melt the fat or oil in a large, heavy pan and in it brown the washed and dried chicken portions until they are golden brown. Remove them from the pan and place them in a large casserole. In the fat frizzle the streaky bacon, cut small, then add the onions, tomatoes, sugar, vinegar and seasonings. Simmer until the tomatoes cook to pulp, then add the tomato purée and a very little water if necessary. Pour this sauce over the chicken, cover the casserole tightly, and cook at 350° F (Gas 4) until the joints are tender (approximately 1 hour).

SERVES 4

CHICKEN IN ONION SAUCE (*E*)

4 chicken joints
1 large onion stock with a
few cloves

½ pint white sauce
salt and pepper

Fry the chicken joints in the usual way. Make an onion sauce as follows. Boil the onion in water until tender. Now make half pint of white sauce with butter and flour, using a mixture of milk and onion cooking liquid. Discard the cloves, chop the onion coarsely and add it to the white sauce. When the chicken joints are cooked, pour over the onion sauce and serve with green peas and baked potatoes or mashed potatoes that have been buttered and browned under the grill.

SERVES 4

CHICKEN IN MUSHROOM SOUP (*E*)

One of the easiest, most straightforward dishes in this book, yet really delicious.

4 chicken joints
1 (10½ oz) tin condensed
mushroom soup

cooking oil
salt and pepper (preferably
freshly ground)

Wipe the joints, brush over with cooking oil, and brown under a hot grill. Transfer to a casserole, spoon the (undiluted) soup around the chicken and sprinkle with a little salt and pepper. (Freshly-ground pepper adds a pleasing piquancy.) Cook, covered, either slowly at 300° F (Gas 2) for 60 to 75 minutes, or at 350° F (Gas 4) for 45 minutes to 60 minutes, depending on the size of the joints. Half way through the cooking time, baste with the now liquid soup. When tender, lift the pieces from the casserole onto a warmed dish, mix the soup and chicken juices thoroughly together, and pour over the chicken. If you are desperately short of time, you can omit the initial grilling process. However, the browned skin makes the dish more pleasing to both eye and palate.

SERVES 4

HOT DISHES USING CHICKEN BREASTS

One of the benefits of modern marketing methods is that chicken breasts can now be bought in separate packets. These delicacies are used in the following recipes, but you can, of course, buy a whole bird or two and cut off the breasts, using the legs and remaining carcase to make other recipes in this book.

Chicken breasts are known as *Suprêmes de volailles*, and we start off with the classic French dish of this name.

CHICKEN BREASTS SUPREME

2 chickens	fine bread-crumbs
2 egg yolks	½ cup cream
6 oz butter	1 (4 oz) tin button
6 tablespoons oil	mushrooms
3 tablespoons flour	nutmeg
¾ cup chicken stock	salt and pepper

Remove the breasts from the bones and take off the skin. Pound the fillets flat between sheets of waxed paper. Season them with salt and pepper, dip them lightly in flour, then in an egg yolk beaten with 1 teaspoon of water, then in fine bread-crumbs. Heat together the butter and oil in a frying pan and brown the chicken breasts in this rather slowly, over moderate heat, for about 3 minutes each side, or until they are golden brown. Remove the chicken to a plate and keep it warm. Strain the fat in the pan into a small bowl, wipe the pan clean, and return to it 2 tablespoons of the clear fat. Blend in 1½ tablespoons of flour and add gradually the chicken stock and cream. Simmer, stirring, until the sauce thickens somewhat. Add a dash of nutmeg, and salt and pepper if necessary. Add mushrooms, drained. Mix 1 egg yolk with a spoonful of the sauce, add this to the sauce, and reheat it, stirring, without letting it boil. Serve this sauce suprême in a sauce-boat.

SERVES 4

CHICKEN BREASTS IN PORT SAUCE

2–4 boned chicken breasts
1 carrot, sliced
1 large onion, sliced
2 cloves
sprigs of thyme or parsley
1 pint stock
1 oz butter

7 medium mushrooms (optional)
1 oz flour
1 tablespoon port
5 tablespoons cream
chopped parsley
salt and pepper

Defrost chicken breasts if necessary. Place the carrot and onion in a pan with the cloves, chicken, herbs and seasoning. Cover with stock. Cover closely and simmer for about 45 minutes or until tender. When chicken is cooked, lift out the pieces and lay in the serving dish. Keep hot. Meanwhile melt the butter in a pan (lightly fry the mushrooms if used and remove from pan). Stir in the flour and lightly cook for a few minutes to form a roux. Strain the simmering liquid into the roux gradually, stirring all the time. Simmer 5 minutes. Add the port, mushrooms and stir in the cream. Heat through and check seasoning. Pour over chicken and sprinkle with chopped parsley.

SERVES 2–4

CUMBERLAND CHICKEN

2 boned chicken breasts
2 oz butter
2 tablespoons lime juice
1 dessertspoon red-currant jelly
3 tablespoons lemon juice

¼ teaspoon dry mustard
pinch ground ginger
few drops tabasco sauce
1 rounded teaspoon cornflour
salt and pepper

Season the defrosted chicken with salt and pepper. Grill for 12 to 15 minutes, turning and basting frequently with the butter and lime juice. Meanwhile, combine the jelly, lemon juice, mustard, ginger and tabasco sauce. Remove the chicken to a hot serving dish, combine the sauce with the drippings in pan, and thicken with the cornflour, blended with a little water. Bring to the boil and cook, stirring, for a few minutes. Pour sauce over chicken, serve hot.

SERVES 2

CHICKEN BREASTS AU GRATIN

4 boned chicken breasts	1 egg
4 slices Gruyère or Cheddar cheese	bread-crumbs
4 slices ham	1 tablespoon flour
	oil or fat for frying

Slit the chicken breasts in half lengthways. Make a 'sandwich' filling with the ham and cheese. Season the flour and dip the filled breasts in it and then in beaten egg and bread-crumbs. Fry in hot fat or oil until crisp and golden brown, then lower the heat and cook the breasts steadily for about 15 minutes. Serve with hot vegetables or if preferred, with a salad.

SERVES 4

CHINESE CHOP SUEY

3 to 4 boned chicken breasts	3 tomatoes, sliced
1 large (16 oz) tin bean sprouts	2 tablespoons cooking oil (or cooking fat)
4 oz tinned bamboo shoots	1 teaspoon cornflour
5 tinned water chestnuts, diced	$\frac{1}{2}$ cup water
4 oz mushrooms, thinly sliced	$\frac{1}{2}$ teaspoon salt
1 large or 2 small onions, finely chopped	1 tablespoon soy sauce

Cut the bamboo shoots into thin slivers. Shred the chicken finely. Prepare the rest of the vegetables. Heat the oil in a frying-pan, fry the chicken, sprinkled with salt, for about 3 minutes.

Remove from pan. Now fry the onions, mushrooms, bean sprouts and tomatoes for a few minutes, turning constantly. Add the bamboo shoots, and water chestnuts. Fry until ingredients are cooked and fat is absorbed. Mix cornflour into the water. Pour into frying-pan, together with soy sauce. Add the shredded chicken. Stir all together, cook for further 2 minutes or until thoroughly hot, then serve immediately.

SERVES 3–4

CHINESE FRIED CHICKEN WITH PORK

2 boned breasts from 1 large chicken	3 eggs
1 lb boneless lean pork	3 level tablespoons soy sauce
3 oz mushrooms, finely chopped	1 level dessertspoon cornflour
5 water chestnuts, finely chopped	4 oz bamboo shoots
	1 tablespoon cooking sherry
	cooking oil or fat

Cut the pork and the chicken into thin slices of roughly equal size. Cut the bamboo shoots into strips (as for Chop Suey), put in a mixing bowl together with the water chestnuts and mushrooms. Add the cornflour, soy sauce, sherry and egg whites, just lightly beaten. Stir all ingredients together thoroughly. Beat the egg yolks separately. Prepare cooking oil or fat for deep frying. Spread each slice of pork with a teaspoonful of the prepared mixture, and place a slice of chicken on top to form a 'sandwich'. Dip the sandwiches in the beaten egg yolks, and fry in the hot, deep fat until golden brown. Serve very hot.

SERVES 4–6

CHICKEN KIEV

4 boned chicken breasts	1 large or 2 small eggs
6 to 8 oz butter	flour
1 cup fine bread-crumbs, preferably brown	oil or clarified butter for deep frying

Skin the breasts if necessary and flatten them with a rolling pin until thin like escallops of veal. Cut the butter, which should be thoroughly chilled, into sticks, place one in the middle of each chicken slice, and fold it over so that the butter is entirely enclosed. Sew with cotton to secure. Sprinkle each chicken parcel with flour, then dip into beaten egg and coat with breadcrumbs. Work quickly so that the butter inside the chicken breasts does not have a chance to soften.

Meanwhile, have ready a deep pan with smoking hot oil or clarified butter. To test whether the temperature of the frying agent is correct, drop into it a small cube of bread which should brown in just over a minute. You may, if you prefer, use a piece of raw potato, and this should quickly fry into a perfect chip. When you have the temperature right, arrange the chicken rolls in a frying basket and lower into the pan. Fry quickly for about 5 minutes until the chicken is golden brown. Drain thoroughly. Remove the cottons before serving and serve very hot.

You may, if you wish to introduce another flavour, soften the butter first, blend into it a tablespoon of chopped parsley and then rechill in a roll shape, or you may chop 2 ounces mushrooms very finely and blend those into the butter and chill before making the parcels.

SERVES 4

CHICKEN BREASTS IN TOMATO WINE SAUCE

3 chicken breasts	¾ cup thick tomato juice
1 oz butter	¼ cup dry sherry
2 dessertspoons olive oil	2 dessertspoons chopped
1 onion, finely chopped	parsley
4 dessertspoons flour	
1½ cups chicken stock	

Skin, bone and halve the breasts. Brown them slowly on both sides in the hot butter and oil. Remove from the pan and put on one side. Lighly brown the onion in the same pan, blend in the flour, then pour on the stock and tomato juice. Stir until the mixture comes to the boil, then season with salt and pepper.

Add the chicken, sherry and parsley and simmer, covered, until the chicken is tender, about 30 minutes. These ingredients are sufficient for about 6 servings.

CHIC HULLOA

2 chicken breasts, skinned and boned	1 cup pineapple juice
1 egg	½ cup white wine
bread-crumbs, seasoned with	juice 1 lemon (4 tablespoons)
1 teaspoon curry powder	1 oz cornflour
¼ teaspoon garlic powder	½ teaspoon curry powder
1 clove garlic, crushed	1 teaspoon sugar
½ oz butter	salt and pepper

Rub chicken with clove garlic, dip in egg and bread-crumbs and fry in butter until golden brown; remove from pan, but keep warm. Wipe grease from pan. Combine the pineapple juice, wine lemon juice, cornflour, garlic powder, curry powder and sugar, and cook slowly until sauce thickens. Place chicken in the sauce, cover and simmer for 25 to 30 minutes. Serve with rice and vegetables.

SERVES 2

CHICKEN AMANDINE

3 oz quick-cooking macaroni	¼ pint double cream
4 chicken breasts or thighs	¼ pint chicken stock, or water and bouillon cube
1 carrot	
1 onion	1 red pepper, shredded
1 bay leaf	½ green pepper, shredded
1 oz butter	1 tablespoon chopped parsley
2 tablespoons onion, finely chopped	1 oz blanched almonds, shredded
½ oz plain flour	salt and pepper

Cook macaroni as directed, and drain. Cover the chicken with cold water. Add salt, pepper, carrot, onion and bay leaf. Simmer until cooked. Fry the onion in butter; stir in flour and cook a few seconds. Add stock and cream, stir until thick and cooked, but do not allow to boil. Add the chicken pieces, macaroni and all the remaining ingredients. Pour into a greased casserole and bake in moderate oven, 375° F (Gas 5), for 15 to 20 minutes.

SERVES 4

CHICKEN ANNA

4 slices ham (thick)	½ cup port wine
4 chicken breasts	1 cup mayonnaise
2 envelopes gelatine	1 cup cream of chicken soup

Soften the gelatine in the port wine and dissolve in the chicken soup which you have first brought to the boil and strained. Lay the chicken breasts on the ham slices, add well beaten mayonnaise to the gelatine mixture and spread over the Suprêmes. Chill, and serve on a bed of green peas and salad.

HOT DISHES USING LEFT-OVERS

HOT CHICKEN MOULD (*E*)

8 oz left-over chicken	or milk
4 oz ham	1 large egg or 2 small ones
2 tablespoons flour	pinch of basil
2 oz butter	salt and pepper
6 tablespoons chicken stock,	

Mince the chicken and ham, add seasoning and basil. Melt the butter and blend into it 2 level tablespoons flour. Gradually add the stock, bring to the boil and simmer for 5 or 6 minutes. Draw from the heat and leave to cool for 10 minutes. Then stir in the eggs, previously well beaten, add the minced meat and mix thoroughly. Grease a mould and turn the mixture into it, pressing well down. Cover with grease-proof paper tied firmly into position, place in a steamer and steam for an hour.

For sauce

1 oz butter	salt
1 oz flour	½ cup tomato pulp
½ pint stock, or milk	or 1 tablespoon tomato purée

Make the sauce by melting the ounce butter in a saucepan. Blend in the flour, making sure the mixture is smooth and does not brown. Add a pinch of salt, then gradually add the stock or milk. Bring slowly to the boil, simmer for 8 to 10 minutes. Heat the tomato pulp or purée separately, and when the white sauce has cooled a little, mix together carefully to avoid curdling. Turn out the mould on to a dish and pour the sauce over.

SERVES 2–3

CHICKEN AND MUSHROOM CREAM (*E*)

1 oz butter	slices of toast
cold cooked chicken	watercress or parsley
cup of white sauce	salt and pepper
3 oz mushrooms	

Make a white sauce with cornflour, milk and a pinch of salt. See previous recipe for method. Blend in the chicken, cut fairly small. Melt the butter, fry the mushrooms gently till soft. Chop, then mix in with other ingredients. Season well, and spread the mixture on slices of buttered toast, garnishing with the watercress or parsley.

CHICKEN IN MARROW (E)

1 medium vegetable marrow	1 dessertspoon mango
left-over chicken (about 12 oz)	chutney
6 tablespoons milk	salt
1 teaspoon curry paste	cayenne
2 tablespoons tomato	1 egg
ketchup	1 teaspoon flour
2 teaspoons mustard (dry)	dripping

Cut a slice off the top of the marrow, peel it and scoop out all the seeds. Boil in salted water for 10 minutes, then lift and drain. Meanwhile, make a sauce by blending the tomato ketchup, mustard, chutney, curry paste, salt, dash of cayenne, and the milk. Mix in the left-over chicken, finely minced, and bind with the egg, previously well beaten. Pack the mixture into the marrow cavity, replace the 'lid' and put in a greased fireproof dish. Dot with dripping, sprinkle the flour from end to end, and bake in a moderate oven 350° F to 375° F (Gas 4–5) until brown and cooked. Make a gravy with some stock (chicken stock preferably) and some brown gravy thickening powder. Serve very hot.

SERVES 4

CHICKEN POPETTES (E)

6 oz minced chicken	½ pint milk
2 oz streaky bacon	4 oz flour
½ teaspoon chopped parsley	lard
2 eggs	salt and pepper

Grill the bacon till crisp, then chop finely. Mix with minced chicken, parsley, salt and pepper, and bind together with one of the eggs, well beaten. Roll into 8 balls. Flour lightly. Make a batter with the flour (adding a pinch of salt), milk and second egg, beating very thoroughly till of a creamy consistency. Put knobs of lard into bun tins and melt in a hot oven. Place a ball of mixture in each, reheat briefly, then add batter to each. Cook until well risen and golden brown in colour.

SERVES 4

STUFFED TOMATOES (E)

4 large tomatoes	cold chicken
2 rashers bacon	large knob butter
1 egg	pinch of basil
1 oz fine bread-crumbs	salt and pepper
3 to 4 tablespoons minced	

Grill the bacon till crisp. Chop finely. Melt the butter, mix in the bacon, bread-crumbs, chicken, salt and pepper. Slice the tops off the tomatoes and scoop out the flesh very carefully. Sieve or mash the flesh and add to the mixture, together with the basil. Bind with the egg, well beaten, and fill the tomatoes with the mixture. Sprinkle the tops with bread-crumbs, replace the lids, dot with butter or margarine and bake in a moderate oven for 15 to 20 minutes. Serve on crisp, fried bread.

SERVES 2

STUFFED PEPPERS (1)

4 peppers (red or green)	6 to 8 mushrooms
1 cup minced or diced chicken	1 oz butter
$\frac{1}{2}$ cup minced or diced ham	bread-crumbs
1 small onion	1 egg
$\frac{1}{2}$ teaspoon minced parsley	salt and pepper

Cut the tops off the peppers at the stem end. Remove all seeds and fibres. Place in boiling water and parboil the peppers for about 5 minutes. Lift from water, turn upside down and leave to drain. Cook the mushrooms gently in half the butter until soft, then chop finely. Grate the onion, and mix it well together with the minced chicken, ham and parsley. Add the chopped mushrooms, season to taste, then bind the mixture with the egg which has been previously well beaten. Pack the filling carefully into the peppers, top with bread-crumbs and dot with the remaining butter. Grease an oven dish, and pour into it enough hot water to cover the bottom. Set the peppers in the dish and bake in a moderate oven, 350° F (Gas 4) for about 20 minutes or until the peppers are tender.

SERVES 4

STUFFED PEPPERS (2)

4 green peppers   4 oz mushrooms, chopped
1 oz butter   6 oz cooked chicken
1 medium onion, chopped   1 (10½ oz) tin tomato soup

Cut the tops off the peppers, scrape out the seeds and the core.
Blanch, by putting them into cold water and bringing them up
to the boil. Pour off the boiling water, rinse the peppers in cold
water and place in a fireproof dish. Melt the butter and fry the
onion and mushrooms, add the chicken and sufficient tomato
soup to bind the mixture together. Put the mixture into the
peppers. Cover with a lid or aluminium foil and cook at 375° F
(Gas 5) for 30 to 40 minutes.

SERVES 4

CHICKEN CROQUETTES   (E)

cold cooked chicken (about   parsley
8 to 10 oz)   knob butter
1 small onion, finely chopped   2 egg yolks
2 to 3 mushrooms, finely   bread-crumbs
chopped   salt and pepper
1 heaped teaspoon chopped

For sauce

1 oz butter   1 teaspoon lemon juice
1 oz flour   salt and pepper
½ pint milk or stock

Make sauce by melting the butter in a pan, mixing the flour
smoothly in and cooking for 5 to 6 minutes. Add milk or stock,
bring to the boil and simmer for 5 minutes. Remove from the
heat, leave to cool slightly, then add lemon juice and seasoning.
    Mince or dice the chicken, using as much white meat as
possible. Melt the knob of butter in a pan, add the onion and
mushrooms. Cook gently till soft, then add chicken and the
binding sauce. Mix thoroughly, then add seasoning and parsley.
When the mixture is cool, add a well beaten egg yolk. Turn on

to a plate to get quite cold, then divide the mixture into short, fat sausage-shaped croquettes, coat with egg and bread-crumbs and fry in deep fat.

Makes about 8

SAVOURY CHICKEN OMELETTE (*E*)

For each person

2 eggs	cold chicken, chopped or
1 tablespoon milk	minced
½ teaspoon chopped fresh	butter
parsley	salt and pepper

Beat the eggs lightly, add salt, pepper, parsley, milk and a few pieces of butter. Warm the minced chicken a little by putting on a plate and standing on a pan of hot water. Melt a large knob of butter in an omelette pan, and pour in the egg mixture when the fat is hot but not smoking. Cook till almost set, then spread the chicken over one half of the omelette. Fold over and serve immediately, garnished with watercress.

CHICKEN RISOTTO WITH BACON (*E*)

6 oz rice	1 pint chicken stock
1 onion, chopped	10 to 12 oz cooked chicken
2 oz mushrooms, chopped	8 rashers streaky bacon
2 oz butter	salt and pepper
2 tablespoons tomato purée	

Wash the rice and drain well. Prepare the onion and mushrooms. Melt the butter in a pan and lightly fry the rice, onion and mushrooms. Add the tomato purée, then gradually pour in the stock or water. Season and bring to the boil, stirring all the time. Reduce the heat and simmer gently until the rice has absorbed all the liquid and is tender (about 35 minutes).

Meanwhile cut the chicken into small pieces. Add to the rice when cooked and heat through over a gentle heat. Remove the rind from the bacon rashers, and form them into rolls. Place on skewers and grill until crisp and lightly browned. Turn the risotto on to a warm serving dish and garnish with the bacon rolls.

SERVES 3–4

SAFFRON CHICKEN RISOTTO WITH PEPPERS

1 large onion, thinly sliced	cheese
2 oz butter	1 large or 2 small peppers
8 oz rice	cooked chicken carcase and
1 pint chicken stock	giblets
pinch of powdered saffron	lemon juice
3 oz grated Cheddar cheese	cooking oil
1 tablespoon grated Parmesan	salt and pepper

Melt the butter in a shallow fireproof casserole and in it fry the onion until transparent. Then stir in the rice and fry till pale biscuit coloured. Add enough stock to float the rice, then cover and simmer gently. Stir frequently adding more stock as it becomes absorbed until the rice is just tender. Stir in enough saffron to colour the rice a delicate yellow. Cut the meat from the chicken carcase into small pieces and chop the liver, heart and gizzard. Add to the rice mixture and heat through. When thoroughly heated, take from the flame and stir in the grated cheese. Season to taste with salt and pepper and a little lemon juice. Cut the pepper in half, remove the stem and seeds, brush with oil and grill on both sides until lightly browned. Cut the pepper into wedges and arrange round the rice.

SERVES 4

CHICKEN CURRY (E)

6 to 8 oz cooked chicken	$\frac{1}{2}$ large cooking apple, finely
2 oz butter	chopped
1 level tablespoon curry	2 oz plain flour
powder	1 level teaspoon turmeric
1 medium onion, finely sliced	1 pint chicken stock

1 tablespoon mango chutney (optional)
1 tablespoon sultanas
8 oz Patna rice

4 slices lemon
1 banana, sliced
a few sultanas and raisins
salt and pepper

Melt the butter in a sizeable pan, add the curry powder and onion and cook slowly together until the onion is almost tender. Then add the apple and cook for another 5 minutes. Stir in the flour and turmeric, then add the chicken stock, and stir the mixture over a gentle heat until it comes to the boil and thickens. Simmer this sauce for a few minutes, then add the chutney and sultanas, and season with salt and pepper. Now stir in the chicken which has been fairly finely cut, and heat it through but do not let it actually come to the boil. Meanwhile, put the rice into boiling salted water, boil steadily for 12 to 15 minutes until the grains are tender. Strain, and rinse under cold water to separate the grains to remove the excess starch, reheat, then arrange the rice round the edge of a warm serving dish and pour the curry into the centre. Garnish with slices of lemon and the sliced banana mixed with the raisins.

CHICKEN PASTIES (E)

Filling

½ oz butter
1 large onion, chopped
½ oz flour
¼ pint chicken stock
6 oz cooked chicken, diced

4 oz cooked potato, diced
1 level dessertspoon chopped parsley
salt and pepper

Short crust pastry

6 oz plain flour
pinch of salt
1½ oz margarine

1½ oz lard
1 to 2 tablespoons water

Filling

Melt the butter and cook the onion until tender, add the flour and cook for a further 2 to 3 minutes. Stir in the stock and bring to the boil, stirring continuously, then simmer for 3 to 4 minutes.

Add the chicken, potato, parsley and seasoning to the sauce and mix well. Allow to become cold.

Pastry

Sift the flour and salt into a bowl and rub in the fat until well blended. Mix to a stiff dough with the water. Roll out the pastry to $\frac{1}{10}$ inch thick and cut three rounds 7 inches in diameter. Divide the filling into three and place in the centre of each round. Damp the edges, and seal across the centre, pinching the edges together. Brush with beaten egg or milk and bake in a moderately hot oven, 400° F (Gas 6), for 25 to 30 minutes, Serve either hot or cold.

CHICKEN AND SCONES

Filling

1 tablespoon oil
1 small onion, chopped
$\frac{1}{2}$ green pepper, chopped
2 oz mushrooms, sliced
1 oz cornflour
2 tablespoons whole berry
cranberry sauce
$\frac{3}{4}$ pint milk or stock
8 oz cooked chicken, cut in cubes
salt and pepper

Scone topping

7 oz plain flour
1 oz cornflour
pinch of salt
2 level teaspoons baking
powder
$\frac{1}{4}$ pint milk
2 tablespoons oil

To make the filling

Heat the oil and sauté the onion, pepper and mushrooms. Stir in the cornflour and cranberry sauce and cook for 1 minute, stirring throughout. Add the milk or stock and continue cooking for a further 1 minute, stirring all the time. Add the cooked chicken and season to taste. Turn into an oven proof dish and top with rounds of scone. Bake at 425° F (Gas 7) for 10 to 15 minutes.

To make the scone topping

Sieve the flour, cornflour, salt and baking powder together.
Mix the milk and corn oil, stir into the dry ingredients. Roll out
on a floured board to about ½ inch thickness. Cut into 1½ inch
rounds.

SERVES 3–4

CHICKEN AND PRAWN PILAFF

2 tablespoons oil
1 large onion, sliced
4 rashers streaky bacon, cut
in strips
2 oz mushrooms, sliced
8 oz Patna rice, washed
1 pint chicken stock

8 oz packet frozen peas
3 tomatoes, skinned, seeded
and cut into strips
4 oz peeled prawns
8 oz cooked chicken, diced
salt and pepper

Heat the oil in a large pan and fry the onion and bacon until
tender. Add the mushrooms and rice and fry for 2 to 3 minutes.
Pour in the stock, season well and simmer for 12 to 15 minutes,
until the rice is tender and the stock is absorbed. Add the peas
to the pan and cook for 5 minutes, then mix in the tomatoes,
prawns and chicken. Heat gently for 5 minutes and pile into a
hot serving dish.

SERVES 4

CHICKEN AND BACON COBBLER (*E*)

1½ oz butter
1 medium onion, finely sliced
2 oz mushrooms, sliced
1 oz flour
1 level tablespoon tomato
purée

1 chicken bouillon cube
¾ pint boiling water
½ bay leaf
8 oz cooked chicken, diced
salt and pepper

Bacon scone topping

6 oz self-raising flour
2 oz margarine
½ teaspoon salt

3 rashers streaky bacon
(diced and crisply fried)
5 tablespoons milk

Pre-heat oven to 425° F (Gas 7). Fry the onion until golden brown and soft, add the mushrooms and cook for 2 to 3 minutes, then stir in the flour and tomato purée. Dissolve the bouillon cube in the water and pour this stock into the pan, blend well and bring to the boil, stirring. Add the seasoning, bay leaf and chicken. Allow to simmer for 10 minutes.

Make the scone topping by rubbing the fat into the flour, add the bacon and the milk and mix to a soft dough. Roll the dough out lightly and cut into 2½ inch rounds with a biscuit cutter. Transfer the chicken mixture to a casserole dish and place the scones on top. Glaze with beaten egg and bake for about ½ hour. Serve with Brussels sprouts.

SERVES 3–4

CHICKEN CLARISSA (*E*)

1 oz margarine
1 oz flour
¾ pint milk, or milk and
chicken stock
salt, pepper and ground mace
to taste

6 to 8 oz diced cooked chicken
1 8 oz packet frozen peas
(cooked)
2 hard boiled eggs, quartered
bacon rolls and triangles of
toast to garnish

Melt the margarine, add the flour and cook for 2 to 3 minutes. Add the milk and bring to the boil, stirring continuously. Cook gently for 3 to 4 minutes, and add seasonings to taste. Add the chicken and peas to the sauce, simmer for 3 minutes then add the eggs and simmer for a further 2 minutes. Adjust the seasoning and serve garnished with bacon rolls and toast.

SERVES 3–4

CHICKEN AND ORANGE OMELETTE (E)

2 eggs	¼ teaspoon grated orange
pinch of salt	rind
pinch of pepper	1 to 2 oz cooked chicken
1 tablespoon water	orange juice
butter	

Lightly beat the eggs with a fork, add the seasoning, the water and the orange rind. Heat some butter in an omelette pan, pour in the mixture and cook until just set. Have ready the filling by chopping the chicken, heating it in a pan with a little butter, some pepper and a few drops of orange juice. Place the filling on one half of the omelette, fold over and serve.

SERVES 1

CHINESE OMELETTE

1 (12 oz) tin Chinese	8 oz cooked chopped chicken
vegetables	2 eggs
2 tablespoons soy sauce	butter
1 heaped teaspoon cornflour	salt and pepper

Strain the liquid from the vegetables, heat it and add to the soy sauce mixed with the cornflour. Cook until smooth and thick then add the vegetables and chicken. Season. Beat the eggs with 1 tablespoon cold water, melt a little butter in an omelette pan and make a thin omelette. Turn the chicken mixture into a small serving dish, and top with omelette.

SERVES 2

CHRISTMAS LOGS (E)

8 oz back bacon rashers

Stuffing

¾ oz butter	parsley
1 small onion, finely chopped	4 level tablespoons fresh
2 oz cooked chicken, finely	white bread-crumbs
chopped	fingers of buttered toast
1 level teaspoon chopped	salt and pepper

P.G.C.—5

Cut each rasher in half. Make the stuffing as follows. Melt the butter and fry the onion for 2 to 3 minutes, add the remaining ingredients and mix well together. Place a little stuffing on each piece of bacon, roll up and place on a baking sheet. Secure with a cocktail stick if necessary. Bake in a moderately hot oven, 400° F (Gas 6) for 15 to 20 minutes until the rolls are crisp and brown. Serve on finger of buttered toast. These may also be served cold.

CHICKEN WITH PINEAPPLE, ALMONDS AND CRANBERRY SAUCE

1 small (7½ oz) tin pineapple pieces
1 tablespoon corn oil
2 oz blanched almonds
1 onion finely chopped
¾ oz cornflour
1 chicken stock cube
2 tablespoons whole berry cranberry sauce
8 oz cooked chicken, cut into strips

Drain the pineapple reserving the juice. Heat the corn oil. Add the almonds and lightly brown. Remove from the pan. Reserve some for garnish. Add the onion and fry until transparent. Add the cornflour, stock cube and cranberry sauce. Make the pineapple juice up to ¾ pint with water. Add to the pan and bring to the boil, stirring. Stir in the chicken, almonds and pineapple pieces. Heat through. Serve on a bed of rice and garnish with almonds.

CHICKEN À LA KING

1½ cups cold chicken, diced finely
3 tablespoons shredded green pepper
4 oz mushrooms, chopped
1½ oz butter
1 egg yolk
1 oz flour
lemon juice
½ cup white stock
6 tablespoons cream
2 or 3 tablespoons sherry (optional)
salt and cayenne pepper

Melt the butter and in it cook the mushrooms and pepper.
Add seasoning, stir in flour and cook for a few minutes. Then
add the white stock, already heated, a dash of lemon juice and
when this is blended, the diced chicken. Cook gently for 5 to
6 minutes, then draw from the heat and mix in slowly a beaten
egg yolk and the cream. It is advisable to warm the egg yolk in
some of the cream first, to prevent curdling. Return to the heat
but make sure the mixture does not boil, then stir till it thickens.
If sherry is used, add this with the stock. The mixture may be
served from a fireproof dish, or piled into a pastry case, ready-
baked blind, on toast, or as a filling for crisp rolls with the soft
crumbs hollowed out.

SERVES 4

TOMATOED CHICKEN ON SPAGHETTI

1 small onion, chopped	¼ pint stock
1 green pepper, chopped	1 (14 oz) tin tomato juice
2 tablespoons oil	mixed herbs
8 oz cooked chicken, chopped	spaghetti
2 tablespoons flour	salt and pepper

Heat the oil and in it sauté the onion and pepper for a few
minutes. Add the chicken to the pan. Stir in the flour, stock and
tomato juice, and bring to the boil, stirring constantly. Season
to taste with salt and pepper, then stir in the herbs. Simmer for
8 to 10 minutes. Meanwhile cook a quantity of spaghetti,
sufficient for four people. Drain and serve topped with the
chicken and tomato mixture.

SERVES 4

CHICKEN CUTLETS (E)

1 boiling fowl, cooked	4–8 oz white bread
flour or fine bread-crumbs	1 large egg
a little butter	salt and pepper
milk	

Skin the fowl and cut off all the white meat. Mince this finely.
Mix the white bread with as much milk as it will absorb, then
mix it with the chicken and mince again. Season with salt and
pepper and bind with the lightly beaten egg. Shape the mixture
into small cakes about 1 inch thick, coat them with flour or
with egg and bread-crumbs and fry in butter. Brown the outsides
quickly, then lower the heat and cook slowly right through.
You can use the remainder of the fowl for any of the casserole
or chicken stew dishes in this book.

CHINESE CHICKEN NOODLES

4 oz egg noodles (fine)	1½ level tablespoons cornflour
4 oz cooked chicken, shredded	2 tablespoons oil
2 oz mushrooms, shredded	2 tablespoons water
2 oz bean sprouts	2 tablespoons soy sauce
2 celery stalks, shredded	salt and pepper
½ pint chicken stock	

Place the noodles in a large pot of boiling water and cook fast
for 15 minutes. Pour into a colander, rinse in cold water and
leave to drain. Heat the oil in a saucepan, put into it the
vegetables, toss them well and cook for about a minute, then
add the chicken, toss and cook for a further minute. Pour in the
stock, stirring well. Cover the pan, lower the heat and simmer
for 10 minutes. Mix the cornflour to a paste with the water and
soy sauce, and add this to the pan mixture. Stir constantly
until the sauce is smooth and thick. Add the seasoning, then
stir in the noodles. Heat the mixture to a high temperature and
then turn it into a deep dish. This quantity makes about
3 moderate-sized portions.

SERVES 3

CHICKEN AND CELERY FLAN (E)

4 oz cooked chicken	of celery ready braised
2 oz cheese (grated)	1 onion
1 (15 oz) tin celery, or 1 head	1 oz flour

2 oz butter
½ pint milk or mixture of milk
and celery stock

4 oz short crust pastry
salt and pepper

Make the pastry, roll it out and line a 6-inch flan ring. Bake
blind (with uncooked beans or rice on greased grease-proof
paper to prevent rising) at the top of the oven for about 15
minutes (425° F, Gas 7). When the pastry has set, take it from
the oven, remove the paper and whatever you have used to
prevent rising. Return to the oven, lower to 350° F (Gas 4) for
a further 5 minutes. Meanwhile, fry the onion in half the butter
until golden brown. Drain the celery, chop it up small, and add
to the onion. Melt the remaining fat in a pan, stir in the flour.
Slowly add the liquid to make a white sauce. Bring the sauce
to the boil, stirring constantly, then pour it on to the vegetables.
Mix lightly and add the chicken, finely chopped, and half the
cheese (grated). When all the ingredients are well combined,
pour the mixture into the flan case, spread with the remaining
cheese and brown it quickly under a very hot grill. This flan
can be served hot with vegetables or cold with salad.

SERVES 3–4

CHICKEN AND HAM PATTIES (*E*)

6 to 7 oz cooked chicken
3 to 4 oz lean bacon or cooked
ham
2 tablespoons flour
6 tablespoons chicken stock
3 tablespoons milk

1 egg
8 oz short or puff pastry
pinch of mixed herbs
1 oz butter
salt and pepper

If bacon is used, grill till cooked. Drain off fat. Cool. Mince
chicken and ham (or bacon) and add herbs. Melt the butter in
pan and make a roux with the flour, stirring well and cooking
gently for 3 or 4 minutes, taking care not to let it brown. Next,
stir in the chicken stock, with seasoning, boil for 4 or 5 minutes,
and add the milk. Draw from the heat, cool slightly, then add
the egg, ready beaten. Return to a very gentle heat and cook
slowly for 3 minutes. Mix in the minced meat, and leave to
get cold.

Meanwhile, make the pastry. Grease some patty tins and line with pastry rounds. Spoon some of the cold mixture into each, cover with pastry rounds, moistening the edges and pressing firmly together. Prick several times on top with a fork, brush with milk or beaten egg, and bake in a hot oven for 10 to 15 minutes until golden brown. Serve either hot or cold.

MAKES 8–12

CHICKEN PUFFS

8 oz flaky or rough puff pastry (home-made or ready-prepared)	1 glass strong chicken stock or wine
2 oz butter	6 oz cold chopped chicken
1½ tablespoon flour	dash lemon juice
6 mushrooms, chopped	2 tablespoons cream
	salt and pepper

Heat butter, add the mushrooms, and cook gently. Sprinkle in the flour, mix well, stir in liquid gradually and allow sauce to cook for a few minutes. Add the cold chicken. Remove from heat, add cream, lemon and seasoning. Allow to cool. Roll out pastry and cut into 4 inch squares. Put spoonfuls of the mixture in each and press together the dampened edges to enclose the filling. Brush with beaten egg or milk. Cook at 400° F (Gas 6) for 30 minutes.

ECONOMICAL CHICKEN VOL-AU-VENT   (E)

8 oz flaky or puff pastry	mushroom soup
cooked chicken left-overs	a little egg and milk
1 (10½ oz) tin condensed	

Make flaky or puff pastry to your favourite recipe or buy some ready-prepared. Cut it in half, roll out both pieces and from each piece cut a 6-inch round. (Use a plate of this size to do so.) Place a saucer or large pastry cutter on one of the circles and cut round, removing the centre. Brush the underside of this hollow ring with milk then place it on the solid circle. Brush the

top with egg or milk and bake in a preheated oven at 425°F
(Gas 7) until golden (about 15 minutes). Meanwhile, heat the
contents of the soup tin and into it blend any scraps of left-over
chicken you have available, chopped or minced finely. Season
well and heat slowly, bringing the mixture to boiling point.
Make sure this is ready by the time the vol-au-vent is cooked.
Scrape out the soft paste from the middle of the cooked
vol-au-vent to give you space for your filling. Pile in the soup
and chicken mixture, and serve immediately. The vol-au-vent
case can be cooked in advance and so can the filling. When you
want to serve the dish turn the filling into the vol-au-vent cavity
quite cold, and heat the whole thing through in a moderate oven.

You can either serve your vol-au-vent 'open' or, to make the
dish even more economical, bake the cut-out circle on a
separate tin, and use it as a 'lid' on the finished dish.

QUICK CHICKEN PIE (E)

8 oz cooked chicken meat	(diced)
1 (10½ oz) tin condensed	1 hard-boiled egg, sliced
mushroom soup	a few cooked peas (optional)
milk	1 to 2 packets potato crisps
4 oz ham or cooked bacon	salt and pepper

Cut the chicken into bite-sized pieces. Pour the contents of the
soup tin into a saucepan and dilute it with half a can of milk
or milk and water. Bring to the boil, season with salt and pepper,
stir in the chicken meat, the ham, egg and peas, if used. Turn
the mixture into a pie-dish and top with crumbled potato crisps.
Bake in a moderate oven for about 15 or 20 minutes.

SERVES 2–3

CHICKEN MUSETTE (E)

8 oz cooked chicken	1 small (6 oz) tin evaporated
3 oz butter	milk
4 level tablespoons flour	½ pint chicken stock
½ teaspoon salt	1 packet frozen broccoli
3 oz grated cheese	(10 oz)
2 oz bread-crumbs	

Following the packet directions cook the broccoli and drain it. In an ovenproof dish place first the chicken meat, well diced, then the cooked broccoli. In a saucepan melt the butter, stir in the flour and salt. Gradually add the chicken stock and evaporated milk and bring to the boil, stirring all the time. Take off the flame, add the cheese, then pour the sauce into the dish. Sprinkle the top with bread-crumbs, dot with butter and bake in the upper part of the oven at 375° F (Gas 5) for about 15 to 20 minutes.

SERVES 2–3

NUTTY CHICKEN

2 oz shelled walnuts or almonds
4 oz butter
1 large onion, sliced
1 small cauliflower
4 oz mushrooms, coarsely chopped
2 level tablespoons flour
¾ pint chicken stock
8 oz cooked chicken
1 teaspoon soy sauce
salt and pepper

Melt the fat in a pan and in it fry the walnuts, quartered, or the almonds, halved. When pale brown and crisp, lift the nuts from the fat, drain and reserve. Meanwhile break the cauliflower into sprigs. Put all the vegetables into the fat and fry gently until tender, about 15 minutes. Next add the chicken, cut into small pieces. Blend the flour with a little chicken stock, stir into the vegetables together with the remaining stock, seasoning and soy sauce. Blend all the ingredients gently but completely, bring to the boil and simmer for about 10 minutes. Just before you are ready to serve, stir in the nuts. Leave for another couple of minutes, then serve on to a hot dish bordered with plain boiled rice.

SERVES 2–3

DISHES FROM CHICKEN LIVERS

SKEWERED CHICKEN LIVERS

1 lb whole chicken livers
3 dessertspoons soy sauce
1 dessertspoon brown sugar
1 dessertspoon sherry

1 teaspoon salt
dash of ginger powder
1 clove garlic, crushed
oil for deep frying

Parboil the chicken livers in salted water for 2 minutes. Make a marinade of the soy sauce, sherry, sugar, salt, ginger and the clove of garlic. Place the livers in this marinade and leave for at least half an hour and preferably 2 or 3 hours. When ready to cook, thread the chicken livers on to skewers and deep fry in oil until golden brown or brush with oil and grill under a hot flame.

SERVES 3–4

SWEET-SOUR CHICKEN LIVERS

8 oz chicken livers
½ cucumber
1 carrot, sliced
2 sticks celery, sliced
½ teaspoon salt
2 tablespoons water
½ cup vinegar

3 tablespoons sugar
1 teaspoon soy sauce
3 teaspoons cornflour
1½ tablespoons oil
small piece green ginger
1 clove garlic, minced
salt and pepper

Pour boiling water over chicken livers and leave for half an hour. Seed the cucumber and cut into thickish pieces. Sprinkle the carrot and celery with salt and leave for 10 minutes. Pour over them the vinegar, sherry, water and sprinkle with 2 tablespoons of the sugar. Leave to marinate for half an hour. Drain, then add soy sauce, cornflour and remaining tablespoon of sugar to the liquid. Heat a little oil in a skillet, fry the ginger and the garlic for a few seconds, then add the liver. Sprinkle with salt and pepper. Stir gently, cover and braise for about 5 minutes. Then pour in the cornflower and vinegar sauce and stir it until it thickens. Finally add the vegetables and cook for a further 5 minutes or until the liver and vegetables are tender.

SERVES 2–3

RISOTTO OF CHICKEN LIVERS (1)

3 dessertspoons cooking oil
1 lb chicken livers, chopped
2 oz mushrooms, sliced
3 onions, chopped
3 celery stalks with leaves, chopped
1 teaspoon basil

½ teaspoon salt
large pinch ground nutmeg
1 teaspoon flour, preferably soya
2 cups ready-cooked rice
2 heaped tablespoons grated Parmesan cheese

Heat the oil in a skillet. Sauté the livers, mushrooms, onions and celery. Remove from the pan and put on one side. In the remaining oil, stir in the salt, flour, seasonings and mix well. Add the liver mixture and the ready-cooked rice. Stir and blend thoroughly. Heat through and serve, topped with the Parmesan cheese. This is sufficient for about 4 servings.

RISOTTO OF CHICKEN LIVERS (2)

4 oz butter
8 oz chicken livers, chopped
2 oz mushrooms, sliced
1 large onion
2 red or green peppers, diced

8 oz long grained rice
2 pints chicken stock
4 tablespoons cooking sherry
Parmesan cheese
salt and pepper

Fry the onion gently in the melted butter until tender. Add the chicken livers to the onion together with the mushrooms, peppers and seasoning. Stir in the rice and fry, stirring frequently, for about 15 minutes. Heat the chicken stock and add to it the cooking sherry. Pour over the rice and liver mixture. Cover tightly and leave to cook very gently until all the liquid has been absorbed. Serve sprinkled with Parmesan cheese.

SERVES 4–6

CHICKEN LIVERS WITH YOGHURT (*E*)

1 lb chicken livers	dash of pepper
1 oz butter	good pinch of salt
½ teaspoon marjoram	6 oz mushrooms, sliced
½ teaspoon Worcester sauce	½ cup yoghurt
1 onion, chopped	½ cup stock
½ oz flour	

Cut the chicken livers into sizeable pieces. Melt the fat in a pan, mix into it the Worcester sauce and marjoram. Lay in the liver pieces and brown very gently. Lift liver from the pan and put on one side. In the pan sauté the onion until soft, blend in the seasonings and the flour. Add the mushrooms, pour in the stock, stir until the mixture simmers. Add the liver and cover Leave to simmer for about 3 to 5 minutes. Take out about 2 tablespoons of the liquid and mix into the yoghurt, then pour the yoghurt into the pan, stirring gently but thoroughly. Heat through very slowly but make sure that the liquid does not boil. Serve with vegetables or on a bed of ready-cooked rice.

SERVES 4

CHICKEN LIVERS ON SCRAMBLED EGG

8 oz chicken livers, sliced	1 tablespoon soy sauce
3 oz butter	3 tablespoons stock or water
2 oz mushrooms, sliced	1 tablespoon single cream
1 small onion, finely chopped	6 eggs
1 tablespoon flour	salt and pepper

Melt 1 ounce of the butter and in it cook the onion gently until tender. Add the livers and mushrooms to the onion and cook all together for 2 to 3 minutes. Stir in the flour. Add the stock, soy sauce and seasoning, cover and leave to cook slowly for 10 to 15 minutes. Next scramble the eggs in the rest of the butter. When just set, remove from the heat, stir in the cream and serve in individual portions with the chicken livers piled in the middle. Garnish with sprigs of parsley.

SERVES 4–6

FESTIVE CHICKEN LIVERS

1 lb chicken livers
1 wine-glass dry vermouth
1 teaspoon Worcester sauce
2 tablespoons lemon juice
1 clove garlic, finely chopped

1 teaspoon made mustard
1 heaped teaspoon arrowroot
½ teaspoon salt
1 oz butter
pinch black pepper

Blend the vermouth, Worcester sauce, lemon juice and garlic, mustard and seasoning. Trim, rinse and drain the chicken livers, pat dry, then place in a basin and pour over them the marinade mixture. Leave for at least 2 hours, but longer if possible. Melt butter in a pan and leave it to brown very slightly, then stir in the livers, but not the marinade. Cover and simmer until the livers are tender (about 10 minutes), stirring from time to time. Strain the marinade, stir in the arrowroot and add it to the mixture in the pan. Continue cooking stirring gently until the mixture thickens. Serve with colourful vegetables, like green peas and baked tomatoes, and with rice rather than potatoes.

SERVES 4

LIVER AND VODKA PÂTÉ

6 oz chicken livers
2 oz butter
1 onion, finely chopped
2 teaspoons vodka

1 garlic clove, crushed with salt
¼ teaspoon parsley
¼ teaspoon thyme
1 bay leaf

Melt half the butter in a pan and in it soften the onion until just cooked but not browned. Add the chicken livers, well rinsed, and cook for 5 minutes. Add the garlic and herbs and cook a further 2 or 3 minutes. Turn into a basin, pound thoroughly. Add the remaining butter, already softened, and also the vodka. Beat all ingredients very thoroughly together. Pack into a mould and chill well before serving. This makes a tasty starter for a small dinner party.

CHICKEN LIVER PÂTÉ (*E*)

8 oz chicken livers
2 oz butter
¼ pint stock or water
1 shallot or piece of onion

1 garlic clove, finely minced
3 slices streaky bacon
salt and pepper

Place the chicken livers into the stock in a small saucepan, together with the shallot or onion and the garlic. Poach for 20 minutes. Drain off the stock and sieve the livers. Melt the butter and stir into the sieved livers. Meanwhile grease a small oven dish and line it with the bacon slices. Season the liver mixture and pack it into the prepared dish. Place in a tin of water into a moderate oven and bake for 30 minutes. Chill before serving in sandwiches or on toast or water biscuits.

CHICKEN LIVERS AU GRATIN

12 oz chicken livers
4 oz butter
2 small onions, finely chopped
4 tomatoes, peeled and sliced
1 pinch thyme
1 pinch dill
1 teaspoon paprika

2 eggs
2 lb potatoes
2 oz grated cheese (Gruyère or Cheddar)
a little scalded milk
bread-crumbs
salt and pepper

Boil the potatoes until soft, drain, mash or sieve thoroughly into a purée. Add the eggs and 1 ounce butter and a little scalded milk. Keep warm until required. Wash the chicken livers, trim and cut into small pieces. Melt 2 ounces butter in a pan and sauté the chicken livers until they are golden brown. Add the onions, tomatoes, herbs, paprika, salt and pepper. Stir, and cook in the pan, uncovered, for 10 minutes.

Pre-heat the oven at a hot setting for 10 minutes. Sprinkle a fireproof dish (greased) with bread-crumbs. Place a layer of potato purée in the bottom. Spread the chicken liver mixture together with the gravy over the mashed potato. Finally spread the remainder of the potato purée on the top and cover with the grated cheese and the rest of the butter, melted. Place at the top of the oven, and leave to bake until golden brown.

SERVES 3–4

CHICKEN LIVERS AND NOODLES (*E*)

12 oz chicken livers, chopped	3 tablespoons olive oil
8 oz tomatoes, peeled and quartered	1 clove garlic, finely chopped
	grated cheese
4 oz peas	salt and pepper
12 oz noodles	

Cook the noodles until soft but not mushy. Drain and keep hot. Meanwhile brown the livers in the oil. Add the garlic, and the tomatoes. Cover and simmer over a low heat for 15 minutes. Finally add the peas, season with salt and pepper and pile the mixture on to the noodles. Serve with grated cheese.

SERVES 3–4

COLD CHICKEN DISHES

CHAUDFROID OF CHICKEN CARDINAL

1 chicken about 3 lb, fresh or
ready-cooked
1 pint packet tomato soup
½ pint water
4 rounded tablespoons thick
mayonnaise
½ teaspoon Worcester sauce

a few drops tabasco (optional)
1 teaspoon lemon juice
a pinch of cayenne
3 stuffed green olives
lettuce for garnish
salt and pepper

If using fresh chicken, cook it by boiling, steam-boiling or
roasting; cool and skin. Remove the two leg joints below the
drumstick. Make the soup according to the directions on the
packet, but using only ½ pint water. Leave to cool, then stir
into the mayonnaise. Add the Worcester sauce, tabasco and
lemon juice and season to taste. Place the chicken on a wire
rack and coat with some of the sauce, making sure the bird
is completely covered. Carefully lift on to a dish and garnish
with lettuce leaves. Slice the olives thinly and use to garnish
the chicken on the breast and drumsticks.

FRIED CHICKEN SALAD   (E)

1 chicken (about 2 lb)
3 large potatoes
1 small (5 oz) tin peas
1 (10½ oz) tin carrots (or
equivalent in fresh carrots)
1 (7 oz) tin sweet-corn
1 lettuce
cucumber

3 or 4 tomatoes, sliced
1 beetroot, diced
mayonnaise
flour
sprigs of watercress
3 oz cooking oil or fat
salt and pepper

Joint the chicken. Roll the joints in flour seasoned with salt and
pepper. Heat the oil or fat, and fry the joints, covered, for about
10 minutes. Uncover, and continue cooking until tender. Drain,
and allow the joints to cool. Boil the potatoes till cooked but

not soft. Cool. Dice them, and mix with the peas and carrots, ready drained. Mix in some mayonnaise, then spread the mixture in the centre of a large, shallow dish (a meat dish is ideal). Arrange cucumber rings round the outside edge of dish, then arrange slices of tomatoes to overlap slightly, all the way round. Place a small pile of diced beetroot at each end. Arrange lettuce leaves on top of diced vegetables. Then, when chicken joints are quite cold, lay them on top of the lettuce and garnish with slices of tomato and sprigs of watercress. Serve with sweet-corn.

This looks decorative and appetizing and can, of course, be adapted for use with single joints of chicken if a whole bird is not required.

SERVES 4–6

ITALIAN CHICKEN SALAD

1 cooked boiling fowl	1 tablespoon tomato ketchup
1 red pepper, and 1 green pepper, cut in julienne strips	½ tablespoon Worcester sauce
	lettuce leaves
3 tablespoons chopped sweet/sour gherkins	3 hard-boiled eggs
	1 (15½ oz) tin pineapple slices
3 tablespoons sweet/sour onions	(or fresh sliced pineapple)
	few radishes
mayonnaise	stuffed olives

Skin and bone the chicken whilst still hot. Leave it to cool, then when cold cut the chicken meat into fine julienne strips. Mix the peppers with the chicken, add chopped gherkins and onions and the tomato ketchup and Worcester sauce. Blend all the ingredients in sufficient mayonnaise to make a smooth salad. Line a serving dish with the lettuce leaves, carefully washed and dried, pile on the chicken mixture and garnish with sliced hard-boiled eggs and pineapple slices. Dot the dish with radish roses and stuffed olives.

SERVES 4–6

JOINTED CHICKEN CHAUDFROID

4 ready-cooked chicken joints	¼ pint thick mayonnaise or
scant ¼ pint aspic jelly	thick white sauce made from
1 teaspoon powdered gelatine	chicken stock
1 to 2 tablespoons cream	garnish

Make the aspic jelly and while it is still warm use to dissolve the gelatine. Whisk the mayonnaise or chicken sauce thoroughly, and add it together with the cream into the aspic mixture. Taste, and reseason if necessary. Allow the sauce to cool. Put the chicken on a wire sieve and coat with the sauce. Leave to set. Cut away the surplus sauce from the bottom of each joint, and when thoroughly set, garnish with peas, tomatoes, hard-boiled egg or stuffed olives. It is better to bone leg and thigh joints of chicken before coating with the sauce. Serve with a colourful salad.

SERVES 4

DEVILLED CHICKEN DRUMSTICKS (*E*)

8 chicken drumsticks	1 level dessertspoon French
¼ pint salad oil	mustard
2 tablespoons Worcester	1 level teaspoon caster sugar
sauce	1 level tablespoon curry
2 rounded tablespoons	powder
tomato ketchup	pinch of paprika
1 level dessertspoon made	salt and pepper
mustard	

Trim the drumsticks and score each with a sharp, pointed knife, cutting down to the bone in several places. Mix all the remaining ingredients together to form a marinade, whisk thoroughly, then pour over the chicken pieces, making sure that the marinade penetrates the cuts. Leave for several hours or over night if possible. Turn and baste from time to time.

Drain the chicken, place the drumsticks in a baking tin. Brush with a little of the marinade and roast in the centre of a moderate oven 375° F (Gas 5) for about 30 minutes. Turn and brush liberally with the marinade from time to time. When the chicken is golden brown, take from the pan and leave it until cold. These devilled drumsticks can be served with a cocktail dip or with a salad. Wrap a small piece of foil round each drumstick tip for decoration.

SERVES 4

TURKISH CHICKEN SALAD

10–12 oz. diced chicken	1 teaspoon salt
1 cup boiled rice	$\frac{1}{4}$ teaspoon pepper
2 oz celery, diced	$\frac{1}{4}$ teaspoon rosemary
1 tin button mushrooms	2 teaspoons onion juice
2 oz chopped black olives	4 dessertspoons vinegar
4 oz green grapes	8 dessertspoons oil

Remove the pips from the grapes, unless they are the seedless variety. Mix together the chicken, rice, celery, mushrooms, olives and grapes. Thoroughly shake together the oil, vinegar, onion juice, rosemary, pepper and salt and pour over the chicken mixture. Serve very cold on a bed of shredded lettuce.

SERVES 4–6

CHICKEN AND CORN SALAD (E)

1 small roast chicken (cold)	5 oz sweetcorn kernels
1 crisp lettuce	1 hard-boiled egg
3 very large tomatoes	sprigs parsley or watercress
5 oz cooked peas	

Carve the chicken into 6 joints. Wash and dry the lettuce and arrange on a flat serving dish. Cut the tomatoes in half, remove some of the pulp and fill 3 with peas and 3 with corn. Mix remaining peas with corn and pile in the centre of the dish with slices of hard-boiled egg around. Arrange the chicken pieces radiating from the centre with the tomato cups and sprigs of parsley between them.

SERVES 6

CHICKEN AND RICE TOSSED SALAD (*E*)

8 oz cooked Patna rice
6 oz cold chicken
1 small onion, chopped
1 (10 oz) tin garden peas
stick of celery, chopped

2 oz rindless mature Cheddar
cheese, cubed
2 tablespoons French dressing
a few chopped walnuts
(optional)

Mix together the rice, chicken, onion, peas, celery and cheese. Toss lightly in the dressing, chill and serve, sprinkled with walnuts.

SERVES 4–6

DANISH CHICKEN SALAD

8 oz cooked chicken
3 hard-boiled eggs
1 level tablespoon horse-
radish (freshly grated)

½ tablespoon vinegar
3 tablespoons whipped cream
1 large tomato
salt and pepper

Cut the chicken into small pieces. Shell the eggs and chop them finely or mash with a fork. Mix in the vinegar and horse-radish and then blend in the cream. Add the chicken, season with salt and pepper. Mix well. Pile on to a serving dish, decorated with sprigs of parsley and thin slices of tomato.

SERVES 3

CALIFORNIAN CHICKEN BASKETS

8 tinned peach halves
8 oz diced cooked chicken
8 oz boiled new potatoes,
diced
4 oz celery, chopped
3 tablespoons mayonnaise
1 tablespoon lemon juice
1 tablespoon minced onion

good pinch pepper
½ teaspoon salt
few toasted almonds
1 large lettuce
few radish roses
few spring onions
parsley

Drain peach halves thoroughly. Mix the chicken, potatoes and celery in a large bowl. Stir the lemon juice, minced onion, salt and pepper into the mayonnaise, and pour over the chicken salad, turning lightly until evenly coated. Fill the centre of each peach half with the mixture. Make a bed of lettuce in a shallow dish, arrange the filled peaches on this and pile rest of chicken salad in centre. Cover with an inverted peach half. Sprinkle tops of peach baskets with toasted almonds, decorate salad with radish roses, spring onions and parsley sprigs.

SERVES 4

CHICKEN APPLE SALAD

12 oz–1 lb chicken meat, cooked and diced
1 head celery, sliced
4 oz olives, black or stuffed
2 oz blanched almonds
5 red-skinned apples

4 tablespoons lemon juice
1 teaspoon salt
⅛ pint double cream
3 tablespoons salad cream
1 lettuce
endive (optional)

Dice four of the apples, unskinned, and toss in half the lemon juice. Mix together the diced chicken, apple, celery, olives and the almonds, cut in slivers. Whip the cream, mix it with the salad cream and salt and mix it lightly into the chicken mixture. Chill. When ready to use, make a bed of lettuce and endive, if used, on a serving platter, and pile the mixture on top. To garnish, core the remaining apple and cut it into rings. Dip in the remaining lemon juice to retain colour, and arrange round the dish. A stuffed olive placed in the centre of the rings will add a colourful touch.

SERVES 6

CHICKEN FRUIT AND RICE SALAD   (E)

1 apple
lemon juice
8 oz cold cooked chicken
4 tablespoons dry cooked rice
1 celery heart, chopped

1 hard-boiled egg, chopped
1 to 2 oz stoned raisins
or dates
mayonnaise
salt and pepper

Dice the apple without peeling it and marinade it in the lemon juice. Cut up the chicken into small pieces and mix with the rice, celery and apple. Add the egg and the raisins or chopped dates, mix with the mayonnaise, add a little seasoning and serve in a large bowl or in individual portions on crisp lettuce leaves, with other salad vegetables if desired.

SERVES 3–4

RIVIERA SALAD

4 oz Patna rice
8 oz cooked chicken, diced
4 oz black grapes, halved and
the pips removed

2 oz skinned and shredded
almonds
3 tablespoons cooking oil
1 tablespoon vinegar
salt and pepper

Cook the rice in fast-boiling salted water until tender, drain and rinse in cold water and allow to cool. Add the chicken, grapes and almonds. Blend the oil and vinegar together and pour this over the rice. Mix well and season to taste. Serve chilled on a bed of lettuce.

SERVES 3–4

CHANTILLY CHICKEN SALAD

2 tablespoons oil
4 tablespoons white wine
juice of $\frac{1}{2}$ lemon
1 pint chicken stock
4 oz mushrooms,
quartered
2 large tomatoes, skinned and
quartered
bay leaf
6 oz rice
$\frac{1}{2}$ oz butter

1 red pepper, cut in strips and
blanched
1 green pepper, cut in strips
and blanched
$\frac{1}{4}$ pint double cream
$\frac{1}{2}$ pint mayonnaise
6 to 8 oz diced cooked chicken
1 lettuce
1 hard-boiled egg
salt and pepper

Heat the oil, wine, lemon juice and $\frac{1}{4}$ pint stock in a pan and add the mushrooms, onions, tomatoes, bay leaf and seasoning.

Cover and cook gently for 6 to 7 minutes. Melt the butter in a large pan, toss the rice in this and then add the mushroom mixture and remaining ¾ pint of stock. Add the peppers, season well, bring to simmering point, cover with grease-proof paper and a lid and cook gently for 15 to 20 minutes until the liquid is absorbed. Remove from the heat and allow to cool. Fold the cream into the mayonnaise, add the chicken and adjust the seasoning. Pile the cold rice mixture in the centre of a dish and arrange the chicken on top. Lay the lettuce around and garnish with the sieved egg yolk and chopped white.

CHICKEN AND CELERY SALAD (E)

2 breasts chicken
1 celery head
1 large lettuce
salt

mayonnaise dressing
2 eggs
4 stuffed olives (optional)

Hard-boil the eggs and leave for garnishing. Arrange the lettuce leaves, washed and very well drained, in a salad bowl. Carve the chicken breast into very thin slices, lay on the lettuce, and add the inner part of the celery, washed, dried, trimmed of greenery and cut into small pieces. Sprinkle salt lightly over, then cover with a good mayonnaise dressing, preferably a home-made one. Chill in the refrigerator for 15 minutes, then garnish with sliced hard-boiled eggs and sliced stuffed olives (if used).

SERVES 3–4

CHICKEN AND PINEAPPLE SALAD

1 large (15 oz) tin pineapple
slices
4 to 6 oz cold chicken
1 lettuce
8 oz lean ham

14-oz packet frozen peas
1 celery heart
few chives
mayonnaise

Wash and well drain the lettuce. Cover a large platter or dish with it. Drain the pineapple. Allow 1 slice for each person and arrange the slices on the lettuce. Chop the remaining pineapple, dice the celery, shred the chicken meat very finely, and mix all together. Blend with some mayonnaise, and pile on to the pineapple rings. Top with a little more mayonnaise and garnish with a few chives, which have been finely chopped. Cut the ham into 3 inch strips, roll up, and arrange the ham rolls regularly around the dish. Thaw the frozen peas. They can be used uncooked or cooked and cooled, as preferred. Take care not to overcook, however, and drain them really well. Arrange in a ring round the outer edge of the platter.

As an alternative, the ham and chicken can be used uncut, and arranged in slices on the lettuce bed, interspersed with pineapple slices. The celery can be cut in strips and arranged decoratively, or served separately together with the mayonnaise dressing.

SERVES 4–6

LEMON CHICKEN SALAD (*E*)

6 to 8 oz cold roast chicken	1 dessertspoon lemon juice
1 lettuce	2 tablespoons olive oil
1 egg	3 teaspoons vinegar
1 beetroot, diced	1 bay leaf
2 tomatoes, thinly sliced	mayonnaise
1 lemon	salt and pepper

Cut up the cold chicken finely, and leave to marinade for at least 2 hours in the olive oil, lemon juice, vinegar, pepper and salt, all mixed together first. Top with slices of lemon and the bay leaf. Stir from time to time. When ready to serve, wash and drain the lettuce, shred fairly finely, and line a salad bowl with a layer. Then add a layer of the chicken meat (first removing the bay leaf), cover with a further layer of shredded lettuce and finish with a top layer of the remainder of the chicken. Spread the diced beetroot and the tomatoes over the mixture, and garnish with the egg, hard-boiled and sliced. Dot with mayonnaise, or spread mayonnaise on the top layer of chicken before adding beetroot and tomatoes.

SERVES 4

COLD CHICKEN SOUFFLÉ

10–12 oz finely minced chicken
1 envelope gelatine
¼ cup water (or chicken consommé)

1 (10 oz) tin cream of chicken soup
1 dessertspoon curry powder (or a little less if preferred)
1 cup whipped cream
salt and pepper

Soften gelatine with water or consommé and stir in the curry powder. Bring the chicken soup to the boil, pour over the gelatine mixture and stir until smooth and quite dissolved. Add the chicken and set on one side to cool. When cool, fold in the whipped cream, season with salt and pepper and pour the mixture into a soufflé dish. Leave to set. Serve with a colourful salad.

ROASTED CHICKEN SALAD IN SOUR CREAM DRESSING

8 oz cooked chicken meat
8 oz celery, diced
8 oz sliced peaches
1 dessertspoon chopped onion

juice of ½ lemon
lettuce leaves
½ cup cooked rice
a few slivered almonds
salt and pepper

Cut the chicken into cubes and mix with the diced celery and sliced peaches. Stir in the onion, season with salt and pepper and sprinkle with lemon juice. Arrange well-washed and dried lettuce leaves on a flat serving dish. Mix the cold rice with some of the sour cream dressing (see below) and place a little on each leaf. Toss the chicken mixture in the rest of the sour cream dressing and arrange the mixture on top of the lettuce salad. Sprinkle with almonds.

SERVES 6

Sour cream dressing

¼ pint sour cream
3 dessertspoons lemon juice
pinch of salt
pinch paprika

¼ teaspoon dry mustard
1 dessertspoon onion, finely chopped

To make sour cream dressing

Whip the cream, add all the other ingredients and mix thoroughly.

JAMAICAN CHICKEN SALAD

½ pint mayonnaise	12 to 16 oz diced cooked
3 oz seedless raisins	chicken
2 dessertspoons rum	2 bananas
2 oz salted peanuts	1 large avocardo pear
4 oz shredded coconut	lemon juice
6 dessertspoons chopped	lettuce leaves
mango chutney	salt and pepper

Sprinkle raisins with the rum and leave to marinate for about 30 minutes. Mix together the mayonnaise, raisins, peanuts, chutney, coconut, chicken meat and one of the bananas, sliced. Season with salt and pepper and pile on to the lettuce leaves. Peel the avocado pear, remove the stone, cut into slices, dipping them in the lemon juice to prevent discolouration. Slice the remaining banana, dip in lemon juice, then arrange the banana and avocado slices alternately round the dish.

SERVES 6–8

CHICKEN WITH AVOCADO

4 avocado pears	lemon juice
6 oz chicken breast	mayonnaise
½ red pepper	stuffed olives
salt	

Slice each pear in half and remove the stone. Dice or mince the chicken, blend with a little mayonnaise, add salt to taste, and a squeeze of lemon. Chop the red pepper finely and mix into the chicken or, if preferred, shred finely and lay in criss-cross fashion after piling the mixture into the hollow of the pear. In either case, garnish with a slice of stuffed olive. Serve as an hors d'oeuvre to 8 people or with green salad as a main course to 4.

CHICKEN LOAF

3 level teaspoons gelatine	8 oz diced cooked chicken
¾ pint hot water	4 oz diced pineapple
2 chicken stock cubes	3 oz seedless grapes
½ teaspoon salt	4 oz diced celery
2 teaspoons lemon juice	

Soften the gelatine in ¼ pint hot water. Bring the remaining ½ pint to the boil, and in it dissolve the 2 chicken cubes. Add the salt, lemon juice and then the softened gelatine. Stir until dissolved and chill until the mixture appears thickish. Then fold in the chicken, pineapple, grapes and celery and pour into a mould. Chill until firm. Turn out and serve with salad. This dish is low in calorie content and is ideal for a slimming diet.

SERVES 3–4

CHICKEN MOULD (E)

12 oz cooked chicken, shredded	2 small tomatoes, thinly sliced
	cooked peas or stuffed olives
¾ pint aspic jelly	French dressing
2 hard-boiled eggs	lettuce

Make the aspic jelly by following the instructions on the packet, and pour some of it into the bottom of a ring mould. Place either the cooked peas or the sliced stuffed olives neatly in the jelly. Slice the hard-boiled eggs evenly. Dip the egg and tomato slices in the remaining aspic jelly and press to side of mould, alternating egg slice with tomato slice all the way round. Leave to set.

When firm, mix the cold chicken with the remains of the egg, peas and tomatoes, and fill the mould. Pour in the remaining liquid aspic. When set, turn out on to a dish, and pile into the centre the lettuce which has previously been washed, shaken thoroughly and, just before required, tossed over and over in French dressing. (See Chicken Flan for method of making this dressing, page 119.)

SERVES 4

SUMMER MOULD

½ pint boiling water
1 chicken stock cube
1 level tablespoon gelatine
¼ tablespoon tabasco sauce
3 tablespoons lemon juice
5 tablespoons mayonnaise
¼ small onion, finely chopped
2 or 3 sticks celery, chopped

1 red-skinned apple, chopped
2 tablespoons peas, cooked
2 tablespoons whole berry
cranberry sauce
8 to 12 oz cooked chicken,
diced
watercress and slices red-
skinned apple for garnish

Add the boiling water to the chicken stock cube and stir well.
Dissolve the gelatine in the hot stock. Stir in tabasco sauce and
lemon juice. Leave to cool but not to set. When cool, gradually
stir in the mayonnaise. When setting point is reached, add the
onion, celery, apple, peas, cranberry sauce and chicken. Turn
into a 6½ inch ring mould and leave to set, preferably overnight.
Turn ou t on to a serving dish and garnish with watercress and
slices of apple, dipped in lemon juice to prevent discoloration.

SERVES 4–6

CHICKEN AND HAM MOUSSE

12 oz cooked chicken
4 oz lean cooked ham
1 oz gelatine
8 fl oz chicken stock
¼ pint cream

8 fl oz milk
1 oz butter
1 oz flour
nut of creamed butter
salt, pepper, cayenne

Make a thick white sauce with the butter, flour and milk. Melt
the butter, draw from flame, stir in flour. When smooth, cook
gently for a few moments, then slowly add milk and cook till
smooth. Leave to cool. Dissolve the gelatine in the chicken
stock. Mince the chicken and the ham, and pound into it the
nut of butter, ready creamed. Season with salt and pepper, add
a dash of cayenne. Blend in the white sauce, then add the
dissolved gelatine, taking care not to curdle the mixture. Whip
the cream lightly, then fold it into the other ingredients. Turn
into a mould to set. When ready for use, turn carefully on to a
dish and garnish with thinly sliced cucumber and tomatoes.

CHICKEN MOUSSE

1½ teaspoons gelatine
¼ cup hot water
2½ cups minced chicken
1 tablespoon chopped parsley
2 tablespoons chopped

peppers
¾ cup cream
1 teaspoon salt
cayenne pepper
stuffed olives

Dissolve the gelatine in hot water. Mix together the chicken, salt, pinch of cayenne, parsley and peppers and add dissolved gelatine. Whip the cream and fold into the mixture. Put in a wet mould. Chill thoroughly. Unmould on lettuce and garnish with sliced stuffed olives.

SERVES 6

CHICKEN IN ASPIC

2 frozen chicken breasts,
defrosted, skinned and boned
pinch marjoram
½ pint aspic jelly

1 hard boiled egg, sliced
watercress for garnish
salt and pepper

Season the chicken pieces with salt, pepper and sprinkle with marjoram. Wrap in aluminium foil, cook for about 20 minutes (400–425° F, Gas 6–7). Meanwhile, pour ¼ inch aspic in a tin of 8 inches diameter. When set, arrange hard-boiled egg slices on top. Add further ¼ inch jelly. Arrange the cooled chicken pieces in tin, pour in remaining jelly, and when set turn on to a serving dish and garnish with watercress. Serve with mixed salad and new potatoes.

SERVES 2–4

HARLEQUIN MOULD

8 oz cooked, diced chicken
meat
1 red-skinned apple, cored
and chopped

1 level dessertspoon grated
onion
1 green pepper, diced
4 tablespoons mayonnaise

3 tablespoons lemon juice
dash tabasco sauce
3 to 4 sticks celery, chopped
stuffed olives

1 tablespoon gelatine
½ pint chicken stock
salad greens

Heat the chicken stock gently, sprinkle in the gelatine and stir, without boiling, until it is dissolved. Rinse a mould, shake well, then place slices of olive in the bottom and pour on a little of the stock, but not enough to make the slices of olive float. Chill in the refrigerator to set firm. Leave the remainder of the stock to cool, then stir in the sauce and lemon juice, whip in the mayonnaise a little at a time.

When the stock mixture reaches setting point, carefully fold in the chopped items, the grated onion and the chicken meat. Turn into the prepared mould, leave to set until required, then unmould on to a bed of salad greens.

SERVES 3–4

CREAM MOUSSE

8 oz cooked chicken meat
(minced)
¼ pint mayonnaise
¼ pint double cream
1 teaspoon celery salt

white pepper
½ pint chicken stock
2 tablespoons lemon juice
1 tablespoon gelatine
salad items to choice

Dissolve the gelatine in the stock, taking care not to boil. When cooled, stir in the chicken meat, lemon juice, flavourings and finally the mayonnaise. Whip the cream, and fold it into the mixture directly setting point has been reached. Pour into a rinsed mould and leave to set. Serve with a colourful salad of lettuce, tomatoes, beetroot, green peppers, etc.

SERVES 3–4

SPRING CHICKEN SALAD MOULDS

1 envelope or 3 teaspoons
gelatine

¼ cup hot water
½ pint salad dressing

2 cups chicken cut into small pieces
4 oz finely chopped celery
2 hard-boiled eggs
½ cup shredded almond and

Brazil nuts
2 tablespoons salad oil
2 tablespoons lemon juice
½ cup tinned, diced pineapple
salt and pepper

Chop whites of eggs. Mix with chicken, celery, pineapple and nuts. Mix oil and lemon juice (or vinegar), salt and pepper; lightly add to the chicken mixture. Leave for 30 minutes. Drain off any liquid and reserve. Dissolve gelatine in hot water. Add to salad dressing and carefully stir in the salad mixture. Place in small moulds and chill. Unmould on to a salad. Sieve the egg yolks over the top and add a sprinkling of chopped parsley.

SERVES 4–6

SUMMER CURRY

1 chicken (2 to 2½ lb), ready cooked
10 oz Patna rice
½ pint mayonnaise
1 head celery
1 small cauliflower
4 medium tomatoes
1 tablespoon grated onion

1 to 2 tablespoons curry powder (according to taste)
salt
black pepper
2 tablespoons cream
lettuce
watercress

Boil the rice in salted water until it is just soft (about 15 to 20 minutes). Drain, rinse and spread in a shallow tin or oven-proof dish. Cover with grease-proof paper and place in a low oven to dry out. Cool. Meanwhile, stir salt and pepper to taste into the mayonnaise and add the curry powder and cream. Chop the celery, separate the flowerets from the cauliflower, wash and drain, and mix these together, adding the grated onion and the chicken meat, taken from the ready cooked bird and cut into small pieces. Blend the chicken mixture with the cooked rice, then fold in the curry mayonnaise. Serve, well cooled, on a bed of lettuce and garnish with sliced tomatoes and watercress sprigs.

SERVES 8

PICNIC PASTIES (*E*)

8 oz flour	cooked green peas and carrots
4 oz lard	1 tablespoon mayonnaise
6 oz cooked chicken	1 tablespoon chopped celery
2 oz cooked ham	salt and pepper

Make shortcrust pastry with the flour and lard. Knead well, and roll out to ⅛ inch thickness. Cut into large rounds about 5 inches in diameter. Mince or finely dice the chicken and the ham, add the celery and other vegetables, varying their quantity according to how much meat you have available. Make enough mixture to spread fairly thickly across half of each pastry round. Blend the mixture with the mayonnaise, season well with salt and pepper. Place on the pastry rounds, fold over and crimp the edges firmly. Prick lightly, brush with milk or a little beaten egg if available. Place on a greased baking tray and bake in a hot oven for 10 minutes or until pastry is a golden brown. Cool on a wire tray. Serve at home with a mixed salad or on picnics with raw whole tomatoes and cos lettuce leaves.

MAKES 5–6

CHICKEN FLAN (*E*)

1 short pastry flan case, baked blind	2 tomatoes, sliced
2 oz rice	6 oz minced chicken,
2 oz cooked peas	French dressing
2 oz cooked, diced carrots	mayonnaise
1 hard-boiled egg	garnish

Boil the rice in salted water till tender. Rinse under cold tap, drain and dry it, then mix with the cooked peas and carrots. Make some French dressing by mixing 2 teaspoons olive oil with a good pinch of mustard and a dash of pepper and salt, then beat in a teaspoon of vinegar. Toss the rice and vegetables in the dressing and spread across the bottom of the flan. Next, spread the minced or diced chicken over the rice mixture, and coat very sparingly with mayonnaise. Top with tomatoes and

hard-boiled egg slices. Garnish with halved stuffed olives or
halved radishes and sprigs of watercress. Serve with lettuce and
cucumber.
SERVES 4–6

TURKEY

If you prefer your Christmas turkey from your poulterer in 'fresh' form (that is, not oven-ready), look for smooth, black legs with short spurs, bright eyes, a broad and plump breast and white flesh. Avoid birds with sunken eyes, pale or light red and rough legs, and long spurs. The best buy of all is a hen of 7 to 9 months old, hens being generally more tender than cocks and lighter boned. You will need to buy a larger 'undressed' bird than a 'dressed' one; allow about 3 extra pounds for the dressing. To prepare for the table, see Chicken (page 32) and proceed in the same way.

Turkey is available in frozen form all year round, and it makes its appearance at table for all kinds of special occasions. For a party meal it is good value, and by use of different stuffings or variations in cooking, can make a most welcome change. Full instructions for handling and cooking turkeys are given in the following section.

These suggestions for cooking oven-ready turkey are designed to help you enjoy the bird at its best and make cooking as trouble-free as possible.

THAW COMPLETELY BEFORE COOKING (see page 31)

It is important that the bird is quite soft before you start cooking, and the best results will be obtained when thawing takes place slowly. See page 125 for full table of thawing and cooking times.

In an emergency you can thaw the turkey quickly by keeping it immersed in warm water. Once thawed, the meat is, of course, perishable and should not be kept unduly long.

THE GIBLETS

Shortly before cooking, take off the plastic wrapper and remove the neck from the body cavity and giblets from the neck cavity of the turkey. Reserve for making stock.

STUFFING AND TRUSSING

Many stuffings are suitable for turkey. (See recipes on pages 127 to 129.) Sprinkle the cavities with salt but do not insert the stuffing until shortly before cooking. Allow a small teacupful of stuffing for each pound of bird. After preparing, fill the stuffing loosely into the neck end of the bird and hold it in place by skewering the neck skin back. If preferred, a different stuffing can be used in the body cavity or an ounce of butter can be inserted instead. Tie the legs securely to the tail with string— no further trussing is required. If you prefer, you can place either a bunch of parsley and a peeled onion, or one or two peeled apples in the cavity instead of stuffing. In this case, cook the stuffing of your choice in a separate greased dish.

Some poultry producers do, in fact, recommend filling the neck cavity only, and cooking the remaining (or alternative) stuffing separately.

ROASTING THE TURKEY

Preheat the oven to the required temperature (see below). Rub the bird generously all over with softened butter. Place, on a rack if possible, in a greased baking tin and cover with a sheet of aluminium foil or double grease-proof paper. Three-quarters of an hour before cooking is completed, remove the wrapping, baste the bird thoroughly and leave to brown all over. (With a large bird it may be sufficient to cut the foil and uncover the breast.)

COOKING TIME

Calculate the cooking time beforehand from the labelled weight which will be found on the wrappings, using the table below. Slow or moderate cooking is recommended, and remember that ovens vary considerably, so be prepared if necessary to give an extra $\frac{1}{2}$ to 1 hour. If the extra time is not needed, the bird can be kept covered in a warm oven until you are ready to serve it.

Test to see if the turkey is cooked by piercing the thigh with a fine skewer—the juices should be almost colourless.

THAWING AND COOKING TIMES FOR TURKEYS

| | Thawing | | Unstuffed or Neck stuffed RECOMMENDED | Cooking |
| | | | | Main Cavity Stuffed |
Turkey weight	Thawing at room temp 65° F	Thawing in refrigerator or outhouse in winter 40° F	Oven 325° F (Gas 2–3)	Cook for 20 mins at 400° F (Gas 6) Then as below at 350 F (Gas 4)
Up to 6½ lb	10–14 hrs	40–50 hrs	2½–3 hrs	2½–3 hrs
6½–8½ lb	14–18 hrs	50–60 hrs	3–3½ hrs	3–3¼ hrs
8½–10½ lb	18–21 hrs	60–66 hrs	3½–4 hrs	3¾–4½ hrs
10½–12½ lb	21–24 hrs	66–69 hrs	4–4½ hrs	4½–5 hrs
12½–15 lb	24–27 hrs	69–72 hrs	20 mins per lb + 20 mins	20 mins per lb + 45 mins
15–20 lb	27–34 hrs	72–76 hrs	20 mins per lb + 20 mins	20 mins per lb + 45 mins
20 lb upwards	34–40 hrs	76–82 hrs	20 mins per lb + 20 mins	20 mins per lb + 45 mins

Traditional garnishes and accompaniments include bread-sauce, stuffing, chipolata sausages, roast potatoes, Brussels sprouts and giblet gravy.

BREAD SAUCE

½ pint milk
1 onion stuck with 5 or 6
cloves

1 blade mace
2 oz white bread-crumbs
1 oz butter

Allow onion, cloves and mace to stand in warmed milk for ½ hour. Strain, return to pan and add butter and bread-crumbs, beating well. Stir until sauce comes to boil.

LIVER AND BACON ROLLS

Cut the turkey liver into small bite-size pieces and roll each in a piece of thin streaky bacon. Impale on a skewer and cook with the turkey for the last 30 minutes.

GIBLET GRAVY

turkey giblets (except liver)
1 onion, sliced
1 carrot, sliced
1 teaspoon salt

4 peppercorns
1 stick celery
1 small bay leaf
cold water

Rinse the giblets in cold water, then place in a saucepan with the vegetables, seasoning and bay leaf. Cover with cold water, bring to the boil and simmer for 2 hours (or pressure-cook for 30 minutes). Strain, and set aside till required.

When the turkey has been transferred to a serving-dish, spoon off as much fat from the pan as possible. Pour some of the giblet broth into the pan, stirring well and scraping all the goodness from the pan. If you prefer a thickened gravy, blend a little cornflour with some cold broth, stir into the pan, simmer, stirring, for 2 minutes, before transferring to a heated sauce-boat.

STUFFINGS FOR ROAST TURKEY

(see also individual recipes)

FARMHOUSE STUFFING (FOR NECK CAVITY)

¼ lb streaky bacon, chopped
3 oz butter or fat (bacon)
1 medium onion, finely
chopped
6 oz stale white bread-crumbs
(2 teacups)
finely grated rind of lemon

1 heaped tablespoon chopped
fresh parsley
1½ level teaspoons dried
thyme
salt, pepper and grated
nutmeg to taste
a little milk

Melt the fat in a saucepan and fry the onion and bacon over gentle heat for several minutes. Add the bread-crumbs and stir, cooking for another minute or two. Stir in all the remaining ingredients and mix to a moist consistency with a little milk if required.

SAVOURY SAUSAGE STUFFING

1½ lb sausage meat
1 dessertspoon mixed herbs

2 onions, finely chopped
1 beaten egg

Mix together all the ingredients and fill into the neck cavity of the bird. Any stuffing left over can be made into sausage meat balls and baked separately.

LEMON, THYME AND MUSHROOM STUFFING

8 oz bread-crumbs
6 oz suet
2 teaspoons thyme

grated rind and juice of
1 lemon
pinch nutmeg

4 oz mushrooms, chopped   2 beaten eggs
4 oz streaky bacon   salt and pepper

Fry the diced bacon and mushrooms in a little butter, mix all the ingredients together and bind with the beaten egg. If necessary, add a little stock to make it more moist. Fill into the body cavity of the bird.

CHESTNUT AND SAUSAGE STUFFING

1 lb chestnuts
1 lb sausage meat
2 or 3 minced shallots – or
1 onion, cooked in butter
3 sticks celery, chopped

2 eggs
½ glass cream or a little milk,
and stock
salt and pepper

Slit the chestnuts, boil in water till soft, then peel and mash. Add all other ingredients and bind together. Fill into the neck cavity of the bird.

BRAZIL NUT AND MUSHROOM STUFFING

4 oz butter
8 oz mushrooms, finely
chopped
2 or 3 sticks celery, diced
2 oz chopped Brazil nuts

1 medium onion, chopped
½ teaspoon salt
8 oz prepared stuffing mix
2 dessertspoons chopped
parsley

Melt the butter in a pan and in it cook the mushrooms, celery, nuts and onion, sprinkled with salt, for about 10 minutes. Stir occasionally. Now add the contents of the stuffing packet and the chopped parsley. Mix thoroughly. Add water or stock if necessary to make a moist stuffing. This is sufficient for a small turkey of about 7 pounds. If you have a larger bird, increase the ingredients proportionately.

HAM AND OLIVE STUFFING

2 cups boiled rice
8 oz toasted bread cubes
2 eggs
½ cup diced cooked ham or bacon
4 oz chopped stuffed green olives
½ teaspoon salt
½ teaspoon sage
½ teaspoon powdered marjoram
a little freshly-ground black pepper
⅛ teaspoon garlic powder
¼ cup chopped fresh parsley
1 small onion, chopped
2 oz diced celery

Lightly beat the eggs and into them add the ingredients, mixing thoroughly and adding a very little stock or water or milk, if necessary, to make a moist stuffing. This amount is suitable for a bird up to 7 to 8 pounds. If you have a large turkey of, say, 12 to 15 pounds, double the ingredients throughout.

PINEAPPLE AND HAM STUFFING

1½ cups minced, cooked ham
1 cup crushed pineapple
4 oz sultanas
1 lb soft white bread-crumbs
6 oz walnuts, chopped
½ cup (scant) honey

Pour boiling water on the sultanas and leave to plump for about 30 minutes. Then mix together with the ham, bread-crumbs, pineapple, walnuts. Slightly warm the honey and use it to bind together the other ingredients.

OYSTER STUFFING

2 oz butter
2 dessertspoons chopped onion
1 dessertspoon chopped parsley
8 oz white bread-crumbs
1 egg
½ pint oysters, chopped
mixed herbs
salt and pepper

Sauté the chopped onion in the butter until pale brown, then mix in the parsley, crumbs, seasonings, oysters, and herbs, Beat the egg and use as much of it as required to bind the ingredients together. Use this stuffing for the crop of your turkey.

ROAST TURKEY DISHES

TURKEY BOURGUIGNON

1 turkey (about 9 lb)
8 oz button mushrooms
6 to 8 very small onions
½ bottle red wine
8 oz streaky bacon

½ teaspoon mixed spice
bouquet garni
butter
salt and black pepper

Sprinkle the inside of the prepared bird with the spice and
seasoning, but do not stuff. Cover the breast with bacon rashers,
overlapping them, and place the bird in a large baking dish.
Chop the turkey liver and heart and place it in a saucepan
with the bouquet garni, the onions and the wine. Bring to
the boil, simmer gently for 15 minutes, by which time the
onions should be soft. Lift the onions from the liquid and reserve.
Pour the hot liquid over the turkey and cook slowly as for
unstuffed turkey (see page 125), basting frequently with the
liquid in the pan. Within 40 minutes from the end of cooking
time, remove the bacon from the breast, place the mushrooms
and onions in the baking dish and continue to baste frequently.
When the turkey is ready, remove to a warmed serving dish,
strain the liquid and place the onions and mushrooms around
the turkey. Keep warm while you put the liquid back again
in the original saucepan. Add small pieces of butter,
beat thoroughly then pour it into a warm sauce-boat and
serve.

FRUITED ROAST TURKEY

1 turkey
2 lb cooking apples
12 oz dried bread-
crumbs

2 oz seedless raisins
4 oz prunes, cooked and
chopped
2 oz brown sugar

1 tablespoon grated lemon
rind
juice of ½ lemon
¼ teaspoon cinnamon
¼ teaspoon powdered ginger
salt

freshly-ground black pepper
(if possible)
4 tablespoons bacon dripping
4 oz lard
1 to 2 wine-glasses cider
(vintage preferably)

Peel, core and slice the apples, mix them with the bread-crumbs and other ingredients. Moisten with sufficient cider to make a fairly soft stuffing, and put it in the turkey cavities. Sew the openings. Melt the lard in a roasting tin, place the turkey in position and roast in the usual way.

TURKEY ITALIENNE

large turkey (12 to 16 lb)
olive oil for basting

Stuffing
turkey liver
4 oz ham
4 oz salami sausage
1 medium onion, finely
chopped
6 oz chestnut purée
8 oz minced veal
olive oil

2 oz white bread-crumbs
4 oz chopped, stoned,
cooked prunes
1 tablespoon white wine (or
water)
pinch nutmeg
1 egg
2 oz Parmesan cheese, grated

Finely chop the ham, turkey liver, and salami sausage. Add the minced veal, onion and chestnut purée and cook all these ingredients slowly in 1 tablespoon olive oil for a few minutes. Remove from heat and stir in the bread-crumbs, prunes, Parmesan cheese, pinch nutmeg and the egg. Add white wine or water to moisten as required, and salt and pepper to taste. (If a sweet stuffing is liked, add 1 tablespoon honey.) Wipe out the turkey with a damp cloth, stuff. Put in a baking tin and pour over a few spoonfuls of olive oil. Soak a piece of muslin in olive oil and lay over the breast of the turkey, and roast in the usual manner. Serve with a plain brown gravy from the giblets, as the stuffing is so rich, and reserve juices in a pan for a soup.

HOT DISHES USING COOKED TURKEY

The following recipes have been designed for turkey meat, but many of the recipes in the Hot Chicken Leftovers section can be used, such as Hot Chicken Mould (p. 78), Risotto (p. 83), curry (p. 84), etc.

TURKEY VOL-AU-VENT   (*E*)

1 large packet frozen puff   milk
pastry, just thawed

Filling
1½ oz butter   1 oz flour
4 rashers lean bacon, cut in   ¼ pint stock
strips   8 oz cooked turkey, diced
4 oz mushrooms, quartered   salt and pepper

Pre-heat the oven to 450° F (Gas 8). Trim the pastry into an oval shape, and with a sharp pointed knife mark another oval ¼ inch in from the edge, cutting halfway through the pastry. Transfer the pastry to a baking sheet and lightly brush with milk. Bake for 15 to 20 minutes, or until golden brown. Meanwhile melt the butter and gently fry the bacon and mushrooms for 5 minutes, add the flour to the pan and stir in the stock and milk. Bring the sauce to the boil and simmer for 5 minutes. Stir in the diced turkey. Season to taste. Remove the lid from the vol-au-vent and scoop out any raw pastry. Fill the centre with the sauce and replace the lid. Garnish with a sprig of parsley, and serve at once.

SERVES 3

TURKEY AND SAUSAGE PILAFF (*E*)

2 oz butter or margarine	2 oz seedless raisins
1 large onion, finely chopped	1 lb pork sausages
8 oz Patna rice	a little fat for frying
1 pint stock or water	1 oz fried, shredded almonds,
8–12 oz cold cooked turkey, diced	or a little chopped parsley
	salt and pepper

Melt 1 ounce butter or margarine and fry the onion gently until cooked but not browned. Add the rice, stir and fry for several minutes, add the stock and seasoning, bring to the boil then cover and cook gently for about 20 minutes. By this time the rice should be just cooked and all the liquid absorbed. Add the turkey, the raisins and the remaining ounce of butter, stir well and keep hot. While the pilaff is cooking, fry the sausages gently in a little fat for 20 minutes. Pile the pilaff in the centre of a hot dish, arrange the cooked sausages around it and garnish with the almonds or chopped parsley.

SERVES 3–4

STUFFED PEPPERS

4 peppers	4 tablespoons bread-crumbs
2 rashers streaky bacon	8 oz cooked turkey, chopped
knob of butter	or minced
small onion, chopped	pinch marjoram
4 small tomatoes, peeled and chopped	little stock
	salt and pepper

Cut a slice from the stalk end of the peppers and scoop out seeds. Parboil in salted water for 5 minutes. Make stuffing by dicing the bacon and cooking with knob of butter. Add the onion and the tomatoes. Stir in the bread-crumbs and add the chopped or minced turkey. Add marjoram and seasoning. Moisten with stock and fill the peppers. Place a knob of butter on top and cook in a baking tin containing a little water at 375° F (Gas 5) for 20 to 30 minutes.

SERVES 4

TURKEYBURGERS IN BLANKETS (E)

1 lb potatoes, cooked and
mashed
6 oz minced or very finely
chopped turkey
1 medium onion, finely
chopped

1 oz rolled oats
2 tablespoons tomato sauce
good pinch mixed herbs
1 egg
butter
salt and pepper

Melt a little butter in a saucepan and in it cook the onion, finely
chopped, until soft but not brown. Put all the ingredients
except the potatoes in a bowl and mix thoroughly together.
Divide the mixture into four, shape into small 'loaves' and
place on lightly greased baking sheet. Cover each loaf with a
layer of mashed potato. Mark with fork. Brush with milk or
beaten egg. Bake in middle shelf moderate oven, 350° F (Gas 4)
for 25 to 30 minutes.

MAKES 4

TURKEY AND CHIPOLATA FLAN (E)

4 pork chipolata sausages
4 rashers streaky bacon
1 oz butter
1 oz flour
½ pint turkey stock and milk,
mixed

8 oz cooked turkey, cubed
tomato wedges
shortcrust pastry using
6 oz flour
salt and pepper

Roll out the pastry and line a square shallow 7 inch tin. Prick
and bake blind in a hot oven (400° F, Gas 6) for 20 minutes.
Meanwhile twist each sausage in half to make two small
sausages and cut. Cut the rashers of bacon in half and roll up.
Place on a tin with the sausages, and bake for 10 minutes. Melt
the butter in a small saucepan, stir in the flour and cook over
a gentle heat for 2 to 3 minutes. Stir in the stock and milk,
bring to the boil, stirring all the time, and simmer 2 to 3 minutes.
Stir in the turkey, season to taste and reheat. Pour in to the hot
pastry case, arrange the sausages radiating from two opposite
corners, and the bacon rolls in a line diagonally from the other

two corners. Garnish the dish with tomato wedges, and serve hot or cold with green salad.

SERVES 4–6

TURKEY TAGLIATELLE

¾ lb green spinach noodles
½ lb cooked ham in large cubes
½ lb cooked turkey, diced
1 red and 1 green sweet pepper, sliced
2 cooking apples, cored and sliced

1 teaspoon sugar
1 (5 oz) tin tomato purée
2 oz butter
1 chicken stock cube
good pinch rosemary
1 heaped teaspoon cornflour
salt and pepper

Cook the noodles in plenty of boiling salted water for 10 to 15 minutes or until just tender. Drain. Toss in a little melted butter, turn into a warm serving dish and pile up round the sides to form a nest. Cover and keep warm in the oven. Make a sauce with the tomato purée and the chicken cube dissolved in ½ pint boiling water. Add the rosemary, sugar, and seasoning to taste. Thicken with the cornflour, first mixed with a little cold water. Sauté the peppers gently in the remaining butter with the apples. When tender, stir in ham and turkey. Pour the sauce over and heat through. Turn the mixture into the centre of the noodle ring.

SERVES 4–6

TURKEY FRICASSÉE

8 oz left-over turkey meat
2 oz smoked tongue
2 oz mushrooms, chopped
½ pint chicken broth
1 oz butter

1 oz flour
2 teaspoons lemon juice
a little chopped parsley
salt and pepper

Sauté the mushrooms in the melted butter for a few minutes, then stir in the flour. Mix well, then gradually pour in the broth, and stir until boiling. Now add the lemon juice, the turkey and tongue, cut into small dice, and the chopped parsley. Season to taste with salt and pepper. Cover the pan and simmer gently for 10 to 12 minutes. Turn the fricassée into a hot serving dish. Garnish with toast fingers or triangles.

SERVES 2–3

TURKEY PIE (*E*)

1 lb turkey meat
2 rashers streaky bacon
1 large onion, finely chopped
2 oz mushrooms, sliced

1 (10½ oz) tin condensed mushroom soup
1 (6 oz) packet ready-made puff pastry (or home-made pastry if preferred)

Chop the turkey meat, and mix together with the mushrooms, onion and the bacon cut in small pieces. Stir in the contents of the soup tin blend thoroughly and turn into a pie dish. Cover with the pastry, thinly rolled, and brush with egg or milk. Bake in a pre-heated oven at 425° F (Gas 7) for 30 to 35 minutes until golden brown.

SERVES 4–5

DEVILLED TURKEY LEGS (*E*)

the legs of a cooked turkey
2 oz melted butter
1 teaspoon each English and French mustard
½ teaspoon curry powder

¼ teaspoon cayenne pepper
¼ teaspoon black pepper
½ teaspoon salt
a few browned bread-crumbs

Separate the thighs from the drumsticks of the legs at the joints, making four portions. Remove the skin. Make 2 or 3 gashes in the flesh. Brush over with melted butter. Mix the mustards, curry powder, peppers and salt to a paste. Spread this paste over the turkey legs, pushing it well into the cuts. Sprinkle with browned bread-crumbs. Place under grill and cook 4 to 5 minutes each side. Add a little more butter on top of joints if necessary to prevent burning.

SERVES 4

TURKEY MUSHROOM SAVOURY (*E*)

8 oz Patna rice	¼ pint milk
4 oz mushrooms	1 heaped teaspoon cornflour
1 large onion, chopped	2 oz butter
12 oz cooked turkey	sprigs parsley (for garnish)
1 chicken stock cube	¼ pint boiling water

Cook the rice in plenty of salted water, rinse, drain, and keep hot. Reserve half the mushrooms for decoration and cook whole in a little butter. Chop the remaining mushrooms. Cook the onion gently in the rest of the butter until limp and transparent. Add the chopped mushrooms, cook for another minute, then stir in the cooked turkey. Dissolve the chicken cube in ¼ pint water (boiling), and moisten the cornflour with the milk. Stir together, and pour into the pan. Continue stirring and cooking gently until the mixture is smooth and thick. Pour on to serving dish, garnish with whole mushrooms and parsley sprigs. Serve with the cooked rice.

SERVES 4

TURKEY FRITTERS (*E*)

8 oz cooked turkey	2 to 3 tablespoons thick white sauce
2 oz cooked ham	a little cayenne pepper, salt and bread-crumbs
1 tablespoon chopped mushrooms	thin slices of fat bacon
1 tablespoon chopped parsley	½ pint tomato sauce

Frying batter

2 oz flour	1 tablespoon salad oil
pinch of salt	1 beaten egg white
1 to 2 egg yolks	fat for deep frying
2 tablespoons of milk	parsley

Mince the turkey and ham, add the chopped mushrooms, parsley, and mix all into the sauce and season. Set the mixture aside until firm. Divide evenly into 6 or 8 portions, roll these

P.G.C.—7

into sausage shapes, using bread-crumbs to prevent stickiness, and wrap each in a very thin slice of bacon.

Batter
Mix the flour and salt together and stir in the egg yolk and milk. Beat until smooth and add the oil. Whisk the white stiffly and fold it into the batter. Dip the fritters into the batter and fry in deep fat. Drain well and arrange on a hot dish. Garnish with parsley and serve tomato sauce separately.

MAKES 6–8

SAFFRON SAVOURY

1 lb cooked turkey cut into
large dice
1 (10½ oz) tin condensed
cream of chicken soup
1 large onion, chopped
2 oz butter
2 oz flour
1 teaspoon salt
1 tablespoon chopped parsley

½ teaspoon white pepper
good pinch thyme
½ teaspoon paprika
powdered saffron
2 apples, peeled and chopped
1 green pepper, sliced in
strips
6 oz long grain rice
1 pint water

Add rice to boiling water, coloured with about half a teaspoon of saffron, or more if a strong colour is desired. Cook until tender, strain and rinse with more hot water, then spread on a serving dish. Mix the flour with the salt, pepper, paprika and thyme. Coat the turkey in the seasoned flour, and fry gently in the butter until all the pieces are evenly browned. Remove and keep hot. Add the apples, onion and green pepper to the pan and cook for a few minutes. Remove strips of pepper and keep for garnish. Add the parsley and soup to pan, cook until blended into a thick smooth sauce. Spoon sauce into centre of rice, arrange turkey pieces and garnish of green pepper on top.

SERVES 4

TURKEY AND ASPARAGUS IN CREAM SAUCE

1 (10½ oz) tin asparagus
spears
about 1 pint stock
1½ oz butter
1½ oz flour
¼ pint single cream

1 dessertspoon lemon juice
2 hard-boiled eggs, sliced
1 lb cooked turkey meat,
roughly chopped
salt and pepper

Drain the liquor from tin of asparagus and make up to 1¼ pints with chicken stock (if no stock available, use water plus chicken cube). In a medium size pan, melt the butter, stir in flour and cook gently for 1 minute. Add measured stock, stir briskly until boiling, then stir in the cream and finally the lemon juice. Season to taste and allow the sauce to simmer gently for several minutes. Reserve a few heads of asparagus for garnishing and chop remainder. Stir turkey, asparagus and 1 sliced egg into the sauce, and turn into a heated shallow serving dish. Arrange a rosette of egg slices in the centre with heads of asparagus radiating from it.

SERVES 4

TURKEY IN WHITE WINE SAUCE

8-12 oz left-over turkey meat
(preferably breast)
3–4 slices of crisp toast
2 oz butter

4 oz mushrooms
Parmesan cheese
chopped parsley

For the sauce
1½ oz butter
1½ oz flour
¼ pint single cream
1 pint stock (made from
turkey giblets if possible)

lemon juice
pinch rosemary
1 glass dry white wine

Place the toast slices in a flat baking dish and on them lay the turkey meat, cut into neat, thin slices. In half the butter, brown the mushrooms, and then place them on top of the turkey meat.

Make the cream sauce as in the preceding recipe, but before adding the lemon juice stir in a pinch of rosemary and the dry white wine. Pour the cream sauce over the contents of the baking dish, sprinkle thickly with Parmesan cheese, dot with the remaining butter, and put into a hot oven to heat through and brown slightly on top.

SERVES 3–4

TURKEY CHOP SUEY

8 oz white turkey meat
3 tablespoons cooking oil
1 onion
1 to 2 cloves garlic
1 small slice ginger, or pinch
ginger powder

2 oz celery
2 oz bean sprouts
1 tablespoon cornflour
2 tablespoons water

Sauce
2 tablespoons soy sauce
1 tablespoon sherry
½ teaspoon sugar

½ teaspoon salt
pinch pepper

Blend the sauce ingredients together and set aside. Cut the turkey meat and the celery into fine strips. Heat the oil in a pan to a fairly high temperature and in it quickly fry the garlic, crushed, the onion, sliced and the ginger, until a light golden brown. Now add the turkey meat and quick fry for 7 to 10 minutes. Lift this mixture from the pan, pour a little more oil into it, heat through and then add the vegetables. Quick fry for 2 minutes, then return the turkey to this mixture, stir and add the ready-prepared sauce. Cook evenly for about a minute, then add the thickening, that is the cornflour dissolved in the water. Cook for a further 2 to 3 minutes when simmering point has been reached.

SERVES 2–3

TURKEY CUTLETS (*E*)

1 lb turkey meat
2 oz mushrooms

½ cup milk
1 egg and one extra yolk

2 slices white bread
flour
brown bread-crumbs

butter, margarine or oil
(for frying)
salt and pepper

Mince the turkey and mushrooms together and season. Soak the bread in the milk, then squeeze and mix the bread with the turkey and mushrooms. Add one beaten egg yolk and shape the mixture into rissoles, either sausage-shaped or flattened. Flour them lightly, dip in beaten egg and brown bread-crumbs and fry in hot butter, margarine or cooking oil, for about 3 minutes each side, until nicely browned. Serve with vegetables or salad.
MAKES 8

TURKEY HASH (*E*)

1 lb cooked turkey meat, diced
8 oz cooked potatoes, diced
2 oz mushrooms
a little chicken stock or turkey giblet stock

2 oz butter
6 to 8 rashers bacon
sweet-corn kernels
parsley
salt and pepper

Sauté the mushrooms and then chop into fairly small pieces. Mix the turkey meat, the cooked mushrooms, and the cooked potatoes with the parsley and seasoning. Add sufficient stock to make not too moist a mixture. Heat the butter in a pan and turn into it the turkey mixture. Smooth and flatten and cook over a moderate heat to brown underneath. Meanwhile make the bacon into rolls, place on skewers, and grill, turning frequently so that they become evenly crisp. Take from the grill and keep hot. Dribble a little melted butter over the pan mixture and place it under the hot grill so that the top becomes brown. Turn the hash on to a serving dish, garnish with the bacon rolls and with sweet-corn kernels, which meanwhile have been heated in a saucepan.

SERVES 4–5

COLD TURKEY DISHES

These dishes, like many given in the preceding section, are designed to make good use of left-over roast bird. Turkey meat can be substituted for the chicken meat which is called for in many of the recipes on pages 103 to 120. For example, Summer Mould, page 115; Chicken Mousse, page 116; Cream Mousse, page 117; Chicken Mould, page 114; Chicken and Ham Mousse, page 115; Chicken Loaf, page 114; Cold Chicken Soufflé, page 112; Roast Chicken Salad, page 112; Riviera Salad, page 109; Chicken and Rice Salad, page 107; Chicken Flan, page 119; Picnic Pasties, page 119. Further ways of using turkey meat are given in the following recipes.

TURKEY AND CHICORY SALAD

1 lb cooked chopped turkey
¼ pint whipped cream
2 tablespoons mayonnaise
pinch cayenne pepper
pinch black pepper

¼ teaspoon salt
2 heads chicory
2 or 3 tomatoes, sliced
half celery heart, chopped
3 to 4 inches cucumber, sliced

Combine the turkey with cream mixed with the mayonnaise season with the cayenne, black pepper and salt. Chill well, then pile up in the centre of a circular platter. Cut the chicory in quarters. Arrange these around the dish. Put the tomatoes, celery and cucumber between the pieces of chicory. Sprinkle with salt and pepper and serve extra mayonnaise separately.

SERVES 4–6

BUFFET SALAD

1 lb diced cooked turkey
¼ cup French dressing

2 oz diced green pepper
2 cups boiled rice

4 oz shredded celery

½ cup mayonnaise

cranberry jelly

lettuces as required

watercress and lemon juice

salt and pepper

Mix turkey with rice and French dressing. Stand in a cold place until required. Just before serving, stir in celery, green pepper or pimento, mayonnaise, salt and pepper to taste, and lemon juice. Make cups with hearts of lettuce leaves on 8 plates. Spoon in salad. Garnish with cranberry jelly and arrange a ring of watercress around the base of each lettuce. This quantity makes 8 servings.

PARTY MOULDS (E)

8 oz cooked turkey

4 oz mushrooms

¼ pint white sauce

½ pint aspic jelly

¼ pint milk

green salad

tomatoes

cucumber

stuffed olives

salt and pepper

Make the aspic jelly up as directed on the packet, and pour a little into individual moulds, setting in the bottom of each a piece of sliced, stuffed olive. Leave to cool. Meanwhile simmer the mushrooms in the milk and when cooked, chop finely. Chop the turkey meat, mix with the mushrooms, season with salt and pepper, stir in the white sauce and the remainder of the aspic jelly. Pour into the moulds and leave to set. When required, turn out on to a bed of lettuce and garnish with sliced tomatoes and cucumber. These individual moulds are particularly suitable for parties, as they are easier to handle than the larger variety.

MAKES 8–10

HAM AND TURKEY CREAMS (E)

4 oz ham

4 oz cooked turkey

½ pint aspic jelly

¼ pint white sauce

½ oz gelatine

1 tablespoon sherry

(optional)

Make up the aspic jelly as instructed on the packet, and thinly coat 8 individual moulds. Mince the turkey and the ham separately and pound them until smooth. Now add half the sauce and half the sherry to each. Mix well and season. Blend half the aspic jelly into the ham mixture and divide between the 8 moulds. Now add the remaining jelly to the pounded turkey and top the moulds with the mixture. Leave to set and when required, dip the moulds in warm water briefly, wipe the outsides, and turn on to a serving dish. Serve with cooked cooled garden peas garnished with tomato wedges.

MAKES 8

SPICED TURKEY LOAF (*E*)

12 oz cooked turkey meat	pepper
8 oz pork sausage meat	turkey stock
1 medium onion	½ pint aspic jelly
sprinkle of parsley	1 teaspoon sherry or brandy
pinch of spice (mixed)	(optional)
pinch nutmeg	2 bay leaves
garlic salt	

Mince together the turkey meat, onion and parsley. In a bowl, mix this with the salt, pepper, spice and nutmeg and bind with the turkey stock. Grease a loaf tin and place half the turkey mixture in the pan, pressing it well down. Cover with half the sausage meat, then put in the remainder of the turkey mixture and finally the rest of the sausage meat. Place the 2 bay leaves on top and bake for 1 hour in a slow oven, 300° F (Gas 2).

Meanwhile, make up the aspic jelly according to the packet instructions, add the sherry or brandy, and when the loaf is quite cold, remove the bay leaves, turn it on to a dish and pour the jelly over. Leave to set in a cold place. Serve with the salad of your choice.

SERVES 6–8

POTTED TURKEY (1) (*E*)

1 lb left-over turkey meat	3 oz butter
3 cooked bacon rashers or	2 bay leaves
3 oz cooked ham or boiled	salt and pepper
bacon	

Pre-heat the oven at 275° F (Gas 1). Mince the turkey meat and
bacon or ham very finely and into it beat 2 ounces of the butter.
Season and spread in a fireproof dish, previously brushed with
melted butter. Place the bay leaves on the top and bake for
30 minutes on the middle shelf of the oven. Remove when
cooked, cool and pour the remaining butter, melted, over.
Use as a savoury spread on toast, biscuits, etc. Keep in the
refrigerator.

POTTED TURKEY AND TONGUE

1 lb cooked turkey meat	1 small onion, finely chopped
4 oz cooked tongue	1 clove garlic
2 oz butter	½ teaspoon nutmeg
turkey (or chicken) stock	salt and pepper
1 tablespoon lemon juice	

Melt the butter in a pan and in it gently fry the onion, until soft.
Take care not to allow it to brown. Pass the turkey meat and
the tongue through the mincer twice, then blend into it the
butter and onion from the pan.

Add the nutmeg and seasoning, and the garlic clove, ready-
crushed. Mix in the lemon juice and a little stock, about two
tablespoons, to give a softish consistency. Pack smoothly into
a dish, pour a little melted butter on top, and chill in the
refrigerator. Serve, sliced, with salad.

If you prefer, the garlic can be omitted, and the lemon flavour
enhanced by adding two teaspoons of grated lemon rind.

TURKEY BRAWN

4 pigs' trotters, cleaned	1½ lb cold turkey meat (or a
2 lb veal bones, broken	mixture of turkey meat, ham,

luncheon meat, etc.)   chopped parsley
1 to 2 tablespoons tomato   salt and pepper
sauce

Wash the pigs' trotters well, and place them with the veal bones in a large saucepan. Fill almost to the top with cold water, add a little salt, bring to the boil. Boil for 5 minutes, skimming if necessary. Now lower the heat, cover and simmer gently for at least 3 hours until the meat falls from the bones. Remove from the heat, strain off the stock, reserve the meat and return the stock to the pan. Bring it to the boil again and boil it fast for about 30 minutes to reduce in quantity. Dice the meat, take the pan off the heat and stir the meat into the stock. Replace over the heat and simmer for 10 minutes, then remove again and stir in the tomato sauce and chopped parsley and season with salt and pepper to taste. Pour into wetted plain moulds or glass dishes, dividing the meat evenly. Leave to set. Before turning out, scrape off the fat from the top. Serve, sliced with salad and pickle.

DISHES USING TURKEY JOINTS

As the price of butcher's meat soars so, too, does the popularity of turkey, which is now readily available in prepackaged portions. Fleshy, tasty and economical, these are as versatile as chicken pieces, and many of the recipes which appear under the chicken sections can easily be adapted for use with turkey meat.

Here, however, are some recipes specially designed for turkey drumsticks, thighs or breasts.

TURKEY PAPRIKA WITH SAVOURY RICE

4 turkey drumsticks or thighs
seasoned flour
2 oz butter
2 medium onions
1 (10½ oz) tin condensed
tomato soup
1 (4 oz) packet frozen mixed
vegetables

4 oz mushrooms, sliced
3 teaspoons paprika
6 oz Patna rice
½ teaspoon celery salt
1 (5 oz) carton soured cream
salt and pepper

Skin the turkey pieces and toss in the seasoned flour. Fry them gently in the melted butter until golden. Lift the pieces from the pan and place on one side, covered to keep warm. Slice the onion, fry in the remaining fat until golden in colour, then add the soup and half a tin of water. Stir in the mushrooms, paprika and salt and pepper to taste. Now replace the turkey into the pan, cover and simmer for 25 to 40 minutes (depending upon the size of the joints) until tender, stirring occasionally. (Thighs will take a little longer than drumsticks.) Cook the rice in boiling salted water for 8 minutes, add the frozen mixed vegetables and the celery salt, and cook for a further 6 to 7 minutes. Drain and arrange on a warm serving dish. Add the soured cream to the turkey mixture; warm through, but take care not to boil. Serve with the savoury rice. (You can also use turkey breasts for this dish, but the cooking time will be reduced to about 20 minutes.)

SERVES 4

SWEET-AND-SPICY TURKEY DRUMSTICKS

4 turkey drumsticks
1 medium (15 oz) tin
pineapple
1 medium onion
1½ oz flour
1 teaspoon brown sugar
½ oz cooking oil

1 oz butter
6 cloves
1 to 2 level teaspoons curry
powder
¼ pint turkey or chicken stock
1 (4 oz) packet frozen peas
salt and pepper

Coat the drumsticks with the flour seasoned with salt and

pepper. Melt the oil and butter together in a heavy pan. When piping hot, fry the drumsticks until they are browned all over. Lift from the pan and arrange them in an ovenproof dish. Drain the pineapple and cut into small pieces. Finely chop the onion and fry it gently in the pan. When the onion begins to colour, add the remaining flour, and curry powder to taste. (If you prefer a mild flavour, add only 1 level teaspoon; if you like it really tangy, use 2 teaspoons.) Mix well, then add the pineapple and about three-quarters of the pineapple juice, the cloves, sugar and stock. Stir the mixture until it boils, then pour it over the drumsticks. Cover the casserole and cook in the oven at 325° F (Gas 3) for about an hour, or until tender. Garnish with the peas, cooked according to packet instructions. Serve with boiled rice.

SERVES 4

TURKEY DRUMSTICKS A L'ITALIENNE

4 turkey drumsticks	Large pinch mixed dried herbs
1 oz butter	1 small (4 oz) packet frozen
1 large onion	peas
1 ounce flour	10 oz long spaghetti
1 (14½ oz) tin tomatoes	2 oz grated cheese
¼ pint chicken or turkey stock	Salt and pepper

Melt the butter in a pan and fry the drumsticks gently for about four minutes, turning occasionally. Chop the onion, add to the pan and fry for a further 3 minutes. Remove the drumsticks, cover and keep warm. Add the flour to the fat and onion, cook for 3 minutes, then carefully add the tomatoes and stock, stirring all the time. Add the herbs, and salt and pepper to taste. Replace the drumsticks, cover the pan and simmer for about 20 minutes or until tender. Then add the peas and cook for a further 5 minutes. Meanwhile, cook the spaghetti in boiling salted water for 15 minutes, drain and pile onto a serving dish. Arrange the drumsticks on top, pour over the sauce and sprinkle the whole with grated cheese.

SERVES 4

TURKEY ORANGE CASSEROLE (*E*)

4 turkey pieces (thighs,   2 oz butter
drumsticks or breasts)   ¾ pint chicken or turkey stock
2 oz flour seasoned with salt   1 (6 oz) tin concentrated
and pepper   orange juice

Coat the turkey pieces with the seasoned flour and fry in the
melted fat until golden brown. Lift the pieces and arrange in an
oven proof dish. Stir the remaining flour into the fat in the pan,
add the stock and the concentrated orange juice. Bring to the
boil, stirring all the time, until the sauce thickens. Pour the
sauce over the turkey, cover, and cook in a 350° F oven (Gas 4)
for 40 to 50 minutes, if using thighs or drumsticks, but if using
breasts, reduce the cooking time to about 25 minutes.

SERVES 4

STUFFED TURKEY BREASTS (*E*)

4 boned turkey breasts   1 teaspoon mixed dried herbs
1 medium onion, chopped   1 egg
3 oz butter   8 oz frozen mixed vegetables
3 oz fresh white bread-crumbs   salt and pepper

Make the stuffing by frying the onion in 1 ounce butter for a
few minutes, until soft, then removing from the heat and adding
the bread-crumbs, herbs and seasoning. Beat the egg and stir
in to mix to a soft consistency. Flatten the turkey breasts with
a rolling pin, and put an equal quantity of the stuffing on each.
Roll up, secure with a cocktail stick. Melt the rest of the butter
in the pan, and in it gently fry the stuffed breasts for about
25 minutes, turning occasionally. Arrange on a warm serving
platter and surround with the frozen vegetables which you
have meanwhile cooked according to packet instructions.

SERVES 4

KENTUCKY TURKEY

4 boned turkey breasts   2–3 oz bread-crumbs
1 egg, beaten   1 (4 oz) packet frozen peas

3 oz butter   corn fritters (see page 57)
4 bananas

Dip the turkey breasts in the beaten egg and roll them in the
bread-crumbs. Melt the fat and fry the turkey pieces until
golden (about 8 to 10 minutes), turning occasionally. Peel the
bananas, slice in half lengthways, and fry in the fat for 2 minutes.
Make corn fritters as for Chicken Maryland on page 57, using
frozen sweetcorn. Lift the turkey and bananas from the pan
and place in the oven to keep hot. Fry the fritters in the remaining fat. Drain well, when cooked, and arrange on the dish with
the turkey and bananas. Cook the peas as directed on the packet,
and use to garnish the finished dish.

SERVES 4

GOLDEN TURKEY BREASTS

4 boned turkey breasts	1 (6 oz) packet frozen sweet-
4 oz butter	corn
2 oz fresh white bread-crumbs	4 tomatoes
1 large onion	watercress
4 oz grated Cheddar cheese	

Gently fry the turkey in the melted fat for 5 to 6 minutes, until
golden in colour. Chop the onion, add to the pan together with
the bread-crumbs, and fry until the onion is soft and light brown.
Remove the turkey breasts and keep them warm. Meanwhile,
cook the sweetcorn as directed on the packet. Drain and
arrange on a warm serving dish. Place the turkey on top of the
corn. Add the cheese to the bread-crumb mixture and almost
immediately spread this mixture over the turkey. Garnish with
tomato halves and watercress sprigs.

SERVES 4

TURKEY CHEESE ROLLS

4 boned turkey breasts	3 oz butter
4 slices ham	2 tablespoons cooking oil
6 oz grated cheese	2 eggs
4 oz fresh white bread-crumbs	salt and pepper

Mix the bread-crumbs with 2 ounces of the grated cheese.
Flatten the turkey breasts with a rolling-pin and 'line' each
breast with ham. Divide the remaining grated cheese between
the four breasts, spread evenly over the ham and roll each
breast up neatly. Secure them with cocktail sticks. Beat the eggs
thoroughly and use to coat the breasts. Roll them in the
bread-crumb-and-cheese mixture until firmly and thickly
covered. Heat the oil in a pan, add the butter and, when piping
hot, quick-fry the breasts until they are brown all over. Lower
the heat, cook slowly for a further 15 minutes, turning occasionally. Drain well and serve with vegetables of your choice, or
with a crisp green salad.

SERVES 4

DEVILLED TURKEY WITH RATATOUILLE

2 oz butter	1 small onion
4 boned turkey breasts	4–6 oz pasta shells
1 tablespoon curry powder	1 (14 oz) packet ratatouille

Melt 1 ounce butter in a pan and brush the turkey pieces all over.
Sprinkle the curry powder over both sides of each breast. Chop
the onion finely, and fry it gently, together with the turkey, in
the remaining butter, for about 10 minutes. Cook the pasta
shells in boiling salted water for 10 minutes. Drain. Cook the
ratatouille as directed on the packet, and serve the devilled
breasts with the pasta shells and the ratatouille.

GOOSE

If possible, get your goose ready-plucked and dressed. Unless a goose is plucked while it is still warm, it is quite hard work. In fact you have to undertake a kind of double operation because in addition to the outer layer of feathers which need to be plucked in the ordinary way, there is an under layer of down. Goose skin is tough, so you will not easily tear it, but there does seem to be a great deal of area to cover. Pluck the upper layer of feathers by taking two or three at a time and pulling them sharply in the direction of the head. For the under layer of down, roll it out with the ball of your thumb, picking it up between thumb and forefinger. Singe off the remaining fluff with a lighted taper or gas flame, being careful not to burn the flesh. Cut the wings off at the 'elbow' joint to save having to pull out the pinions.

To remove the head, cut through the neck skin about two inches above the shoulders. Now draw the skin back and cut the neck as close to the body of the bird as you possibly can. To take off the feet, cut round the heel joint, break the bone and remove the paddles and draw the tendons as for other birds. These tendons are quite hard to draw out; there are about six in each leg and each needs to be pulled out singly.

To draw the bird, open it down from the breast bone to the vent. In the resulting hole, insert your fingers and take hold of the gizzard, entrails, lungs, windpipe and gullet, and any fat that you can draw out. Keep the giblets (that is the heart, gizzard and liver) and, of course, the fat, and then discard the remaining entrails. Take great care, as when drawing other birds, not to puncture the gall-bladder. Having made sure that the bird is empty and clean, wipe it thoroughly with a clean, damp cloth.

After stuffing the bird (see below), truss it ready for roasting. Tuck the tail into the vent end and secure it with a small skewer. Pass other skewers through the body in two or three places and then wind string round the skewers to keep them in position. Do not pass the string over the breast of the goose. Tuck the neck skin in under the string.

If using oven-ready frozen goose, read the important note on thawing poultry on page 31.

STUFFINGS FOR ROAST GOOSE

As goose, like duck, possesses a great deal of fat, most of the stuffings suggested for duck are equally suitable for goose, but remember that the goose has a very large cavity and therefore it will be necessary to make at least double the quantity.

SAGE AND ONION STUFFING

4 oz bread-crumbs
4 onions, peeled and finely chopped
1 dessertspoon sage

1 oz butter
1 egg
stock or water
salt and pepper

Simmer the onions in a little water or stock until tender. Add the sage, bread-crumbs, butter, seasoning and mix well. Then add sufficient beaten egg to bind into a firm stuffing.

CELERY AND APPLE STUFFING

3 oz bread-crumbs
2 onions, chopped
2 or 3 oz bacon
4 or 5 tablespoons chopped celery

4 medium cooking apples
1½ tablespoons chopped parsley
salt and pepper

Dice the bacon and brown it in its own fat. Lift from the pan and in the residual fat gently cook the onions and celery. Cook for 5 minutes and remove. Still using the same fat, fry the apples, diced, until they are tender and brown. Now mix these cooked ingredients together with the bread-crumbs, herbs, seasoning and use to stuff the bird.

TANGERINE AND CHESTNUT STUFFING

2 oz butter
2 oz diced celery (with some leaves)
3 tangerines
4 oz cooked, chopped chestnuts

2 cups cooked rice
8 oz packet sage and onion stuffing mix
½ cup stock or water

Melt the butter in a pan and in it cook the celery over a medium heat for about 8 minutes. Peel the tangerines, remove the white membranes. Cut the sections into halves and take out the pips. Mix together the tangerines, stuffing mix, chestnuts, seasonings, rice and stock, then add the cooked celery and butter, and mix together lightly with a fork. Add a little more stock if necessary.

APPLE AND POTATO STUFFING

8 oz mashed potato
2 large cooking apples
2 medium onions
½ teaspoon sage

1 level teaspoon thyme (powdered)
salt and pepper

Chop the apples and mix with the powdered herbs. Parboil the onions, chop and add to all the other ingredients. Season to taste. Bind with a little beaten egg or milk.

PRUNE AND RAISIN STUFFING

1 lb prunes
3 tablespoons raisins
4 large cooking apples

1 level teaspoon salt
¼ teaspoon pepper
1 egg

Soak the prunes for at least 2 hours, covering with boiling water, then stone and chop them and mix with the apples, peeled, cored and chopped, and the raisins, rinsed. Add the seasoning and bind with the egg, well beaten.

P.G.C.—8

APRICOT STUFFING

Especially suitable for roast wild goose.

2 oz butter
1 small onion, chopped
2 medium cooking apples,
chopped

4 oz dried apricots, chopped
12 oz soft white bread-crumbs
½ teaspoon salt
good pinch pepper

In a large saucepan, melt the butter and in it cook the onion until tender. Now stir in the chopped apple and apricots, the bread-crumbs, salt and pepper, and mix thoroughly together.

WALNUT STUFFING

4 oz bread-crumbs
1 teaspoon powdered mixed
herbs
2 medium onions, finely
chopped
1 oz butter

2 large cooking apples
4 oz pork sausage meat
2 dozen walnuts
1 egg
a little milk

Fry the onions till soft and pale gold in the melted butter. Peel the apples and shell the walnuts, chop both and mix all the ingredients together. Bind with the beaten egg and add as much as necessary to form a firm yet manageable stuffing.

ROAST GOOSE DISHES

Roasting is by far the best way of cooking goose, and variety can be supplied from time to time by using different stuffings. The foregoing recipes giving various stuffings will indicate how this can be done. Below is the basic roasting method followed by a few variations, using particular stuffings for particular effect.

ROAST GOOSE

Sprinkle the prepared and stuffed bird with salt and place on a trivet in a roasting pan, on its side. Place on the bird a little of the fat reserved from drawing or about 2 tablespoons of melted butter or margarine. Goose makes its own fat for cooking, so no more than this is necessary. Cover with foil and roast at 400° F (Gas 6) for the first hour, then turn the bird on its other side, baste well, and lower the heat to 375° F (Gas 5). Allow 15 to 18 minutes per pound and baste frequently for the rest of the cooking time. Turn the bird with breast uppermost for the last 30 minutes and remove the foil so that the breast will become nicely browned. Spoon off some of the excess fat when you are basting and reserve in a basin. If the pan tends to get a little too brown, add half a cup of hot water to the juices.

An alternative method of cooking is to roast in a moderate oven 350° F (Gas 4) throughout, allowing 25 to 30 minutes per pound. Remove the foil for the last half hour as above. When the bird is cooked, the legs should move up and down quite freely. To confirm that it is ready, cut a leg free, press it out and down and if the hip joint dislocates easily the bird is cooked.

Pour off the goose-grease into a bowl. Scatter a tablespoon of flour into the remaining juices in the pan, stir thoroughly and put back over the heat. Pour in stock made from the giblets which have previously been simmered. Boil the gravy until smooth. Serve with apple sauce.

APPLE SAUCE

1½ lb cooking apples, cored and chopped	2 oz butter
2 medium onions, finely chopped	2 oz sugar
	4 cloves
	1 tablespoon cooking sherry

Melt the butter in a saucepan and in it cook the onion until it begins to go transparent. Then add the apple. Sprinkle over the sugar, stir constantly, and cook slowly until the apple softens. Add the cloves and finally the cooking sherry, a tablespoon or more if liked.

DANISH ROAST GOOSE

1 goose	1 teaspoon sugar per cup of
salt	stuffing
prunes	red-current jelly
cooking apples	

The amount of stuffing used will depend on the size of the goose.
Allow for each pound of the bird, ready-to-cook weight, one cup
of mixed apples and prunes. Soak the prunes for at least 2 hours,
then drain and take out the stones. Peel, core and slice the apples,
mix together and sprinkle with the sugar. Sprinkle the inside of
the goose cavity with salt, then fill with the prepared fruit. Truss
and roast as above. Into the final gravy stir a tablespoon or two
of red current jelly.

GOOSE WITH RED CABBAGE

1 goose	salt
2 lb cooking apples	pinch cinnamon
12 oz sultanas and currants	a little butter
(mixed)	1 medium red cabbage
4 oz fine bread-crumbs	6 smoked sausages
2 eggs	3 tablespoons vinegar

Make a stuffing by mixing the apples, peeled, cored and cut into
pieces, with the fruit, bread-crumbs, cinnamon, salt and eggs,
well beaten. Place this stuffing into the prepared bird, and place
it on a trivet in a baking tin. Add $\frac{1}{2}$ pint of water to the tin and
spread a little butter over the bird. Roast in the usual way (see
page 159), basting frequently.

Meanwhile shred the cabbage, wash and dry it, and then
simmer in a very little stock until almost tender. Now add the
sausages, cut into pieces, and when the cabbage is quite soft,
stir in the vinegar. When the goose is cooked serve on a dish
with the cabbage and sausages and accompanied by boiled or
sautéed potatoes. For the gravy, pour off the goose fat and stir
the liquid from the cabbage into the remaining juices. Bring to
the boil, strain and serve.

RUSSIAN ROAST GOOSE

1 goose   1 medium head celery
½ teaspoon carraway seeds   3 to 4 onions, chopped
2 lb cooking apples   salt

Rub the prepared bird with salt, inside and out. Sprinkle the
carraway seeds into the cavity, then stuff with the apples left
whole, the celery and onions. Roast in the usual way (see
page 159).

GIBLET PIE (*E*)

1 set goose giblets   6 oz puff or shortcrust pastry
1 lb good quality braising   milk for glazing
steak   bouquet garni
1 onion, sliced   salt and pepper

Place the washed giblets in a saucepan together with the onion,
the bouquet garni and seasonings, and cover with cold water.
Simmer on a low heat for about 2 hours. Leave to cool. Meanwhile mince the steak or cut it very finely, season, and when the
giblets are cool, place alternate layers of meat and chopped
giblets in a pie-dish which should be just large enough to take
the quantity. Strain the giblet stock and put into the dish until
about three-quarters full. Make puff or short pastry based on
6 ounces flour, roll out, cover the pie-dish, glaze with a little
milk, and bake in a hot oven 425° F (Gas 7) for 20 minutes, then
lower the heat to 350° F (Gas 4) and continue cooking for about
a further 50 minutes. Use the remaining goose giblet stock to
make a gravy.

GOOSE LIVER PÂTÉ

6 oz goose liver   bouquet garni
3 oz butter   freshly-ground black pepper
1 small onion, finely chopped   1 dessertspoon brandy
⅛ teaspoon grated nutmeg

Melt 1 ounce of butter in a saucepan and in it fry the onion until it begins to turn golden brown. Now add the goose liver, herbs, a little salt, pepper, nutmeg and fry slowly for 4 minutes, turning once. Leave to cool, then pass twice through a mincer and finally through a fine sieve. Cream the remaining butter, work it into the liver mixture, and finally add the brandy. Pack the paté into a china jar and seal with clarified butter. Keep in a refrigerator, but not for more than a few days.

DUCK

Duck (or duckling) should be eaten before it is 12 months old. After that it is liable to be tough. When buying a non-prepared bird, watch out for bright yellow feet and a bill which is soft enough to bend back easily. The breast flesh should be white and meaty. To dress, follow the instructions as for chicken on page 32.

Before cooking a frozen (oven-ready) bird, make sure that it is *completely thawed out* – 5 to 8 hours, or preferably left overnight. If it is necessary to thaw the bird quickly, submerge it (wrapped) in cold water for about 2 hours. (See note on washing frozen poultry, page 33.)

ROAST DUCK

Pre-heat your oven to 350° F (Gas 4). Remove the giblets and use them for making stock. Rinse the duckling, dry, and stuff in whatever way you choose. Alternatively, insert into the cavity one whole washed orange. Always stuff the duck from the vent end. Brush the bird with oil or melted butter and cook in a roasting tin, allowing 30 minutes to the pound. As duck carries a good deal of fat, it is not necessary to baste.

STUFFINGS FOR ROAST DUCK

APPLE AND CELERY STUFFING

2 oz bacon or salt pork
2 onions, chopped
2 large sticks celery, chopped
4 medium cooking apples
3 oz white bread-crumbs
2 tablespoons chopped parsley
a little sugar to taste
salt and pepper

Rind the bacon, chop it (or the salt pork) and place in a stout frying-pan to draw off the fat. Cook the bacon or pork in its own fat for about 3 minutes until brown, then lift with a slotted spoon and reserve. Fry the onion in the pork fat together with the celery, for about 5 minutes; then remove from the pan. Meanwhile peel and dice the apples, now add them to the same fat and fry until tender and brown. Mix all these ingredients and the crumbs and seasonings together, adding a little melted butter to bind if necessary.

ORANGE AND HERB STUFFING

4 tablespoons white bread-crumbs
2 tablespoons chopped herbs (parsley, thyme, chives, marjoram)
2 tablespoons finely chopped onion

1 to 1½ oz butter
juice and grated rind of 1 large orange
1 egg
salt and pepper

Mix in a bowl the crumbs, herbs and seasoning. Melt the butter in a pan and in it soften the onion, but do not let it brown. Add the cooked onion to the herb mixture, together with the grated orange rind and juice. Bind with the egg, well beaten, and if the mixture is still too dry and crumbly, add a little extra orange juice.

CRANBERRY STUFFING

½ lb fresh white bread-crumbs
¾ lb prunes, pre-soaked
2 large apples, peeled and diced
3 oz almonds, blanched and chopped

2 tablespoons whole berry cranberry sauce
grated rind and juice of 1 lemon
1 egg
1 tablespoon corn oil

Place bread-crumbs in a bowl. Add the roughly chopped prunes, apple, almonds, cranberry sauce and lemon. Bind together with the beaten eggs and corn oil.

ORANGE APRICOT STUFFING

3 dessertspoons oil
1 medium onion, finely
chopped
3 or 4 celery stalks and leaves,
finely chopped
2 oz mushrooms, thinly sliced
2 oranges

8 oz dried apricots
3 cups ready-cooked rice
(preferably brown)
½ teaspoon salt
½ teaspoon thyme
pinch of cinnamon
pinch of mace

Heat the oil and in it sauté the onion, celery and the mushrooms.
Grate the rind from the two oranges and squeeze the juice to
make up to one cupful. Chop the dried apricots finely and mix
together with all the other ingredients. Add the seasonings and
spices and the ready-cooked rice. Mix all ingredients thoroughly
together.

SWEDISH STUFFING

2 cups ready-cooked rice
½ cup sultanas or seedless
raisins
pinch ground cardamom
1 piece onion

1 teaspoon grated orange rind
½ teaspoon salt
2 dessertspoons melted butter
1 apple

Peel and grate the apple, chop the onion very finely. Wash and
drain the sultanas or raisins and mix together with the ready-
cooked rice, orange rind, onion, melted butter, apple and
seasonings. Blend all ingredients lightly with a fork, and stuff
into the body cavity of the duck.

HOT DUCK DISHES

Duck is delicious when combined with wine and fruit. Dishes such as Duck with Peaches, Duck with Apricots, Luxury Duck à l'Orange and Duck with Cherries are all worthy of a dinner-party. Nevertheless, a number of more economical duck dishes are included in this section.

ROAST DUCKLING WITH APPLE AND ONION SAUCE

1 duckling (about 4 lb)
1 peeled onion or sage and onion stuffing

1 oz softened butter or dripping
salt and pepper

Prepare a moderately slow oven, 325° F (Gas 3). Remove giblets from the body cavity of the thawed duck and wipe with a damp cloth (see note about washing poultry, p. 33). Season inside and out with salt and pepper. Spread the bird all over with softened butter or dripping. Insert into body cavity the stuffing or peeled onion and the liver. Place in shallow roasting tin. Cook, allowing 30 minutes per pound. Drain off surplus fat and make gravy with giblet stock. Serve with apple and onion sauce, orange salad, green peas or braised celery.

Apple and onion sauce
1 lb apples
2 tablespoons sherry or water
1 tablespoon chopped onion

½ oz butter
1 tablespoon brown or castor sugar

Peel, core and slice the apples, thinly. Place in a saucepan with the sherry or water and chopped onion. Cover closely. Simmer gently, stirring occasionally till reduced to a pulp. Add butter and sugar. Stir till butter and sugar are melted. Serve in a heated sauce-boat.

ROAST DUCK A L'ORANGE

1 duck (about 5 lb)	¾ pint stock (made from bird
2 large oranges	giblets)
2 level teaspoons arrowroot	2 teaspoons sherry (optional)
	2 teaspoons lemon juice

Roast the duck at 350° F (Gas 4) allowing 30 minutes per pound, or at 400° F (Gas 6) allowing 20 minutes per pound. Meanwhile wash the oranges, peel off the thin outer skins and blanch in boiling water. Cut the skin into very thin strips. Mix a little cold stock into the arrowroot, then boil the remainder and stir in the blended arrowroot, cooking for 3 minutes and stirring all the time. Add the lemon juice and juice of the two peeled oranges. Next add the sherry and finally the shredded orange peel. Place the cooked duck on a serving dish and pour over it this orange sauce. Serve with vegetables and, if possible, an orange salad made from oranges skinned and thinly sliced and sprinkled with chopped mint and French dressing.

SERVES 3–4

DUCK WITH GOOSEBERRY SAUCE

1 duck (about 5 lb)	a little butter
½ pint gooseberry purée	1 teaspoon lemon juice
1 tablespoon sugar	1 wine glass sherry

Roast the duck towards the top of the oven until tender. Baste it about every 15 or 20 minutes with the fat that runs out. Meanwhile mix together the gooseberry purée, sugar, lemon juice and butter (about a tablespoonful), and heat slowly.

Just before you are ready to serve, add the sherry to this sauce. Do not pour it over the bird, but pass it separately.

SERVES 3–4

CRANBERRY DUCKLING

1 duck (5 to 6 lb)	½ oz cornflour
cranberry stuffing (see page 166)	4 oz sugar

1 lb fresh cranberries   ¼ pint orange juice
¼ pint water   1 orange

Stuff the duck with the cranberry stuffing and roast until almost
tender and the skin a light brown. Meanwhile, make the sauce
by placing the water, sugar, cranberries, cornflour and orange
juice in a saucepan. Bring it to the boil, stirring constantly, and
cook over a medium heat until the liquid is clear and syrupy
(about 5 minutes). Remove from the heat and add the orange,
unpeeled, but cut into thick wedges (about 6). Remove the
duck from the oven and transfer it to a deep casserole. Pour the
sauce over the bird, cover, and return to the oven for about a
further 20 minutes, or until the duck feels tender when pricked.
Baste the duck once during this cooking period.

SERVES 3–4

NORWEGIAN PRUNE-STUFFED DUCK

1 duck (4 to 5 lb)   small carton (4 oz) cream
5 apples, peeled and diced   ¾ pint giblet gravy
15 prunes   a little blackcurrant juice
3 tablespoons flour   salt and pepper

Season and prepare the duck for roasting in the usual way. Stuff
the apples and the prunes into the vent end. Sew the bird up
and roast until crisp and tender. Place on a serving dish when
cooked, pour off the gravy and skim the fat from it. Now add a
little water and stir in the flour to thicken. Next add the giblet
gravy, cream and a little blackcurrant juice (optional). Serve
the bird with baked or fried potatoes and with more cooked
prunes and apples if you wish. Serve the sauce separately.

SERVES 3–4

DUCKLING WITH LIVER STUFFING

1 duckling (about 5 lb)   ¾ pint brown sauce
cooking fat   1 orange

Stuffing
1 chicken liver   ½ teaspoon parsley
1 duckling liver   ¼ teaspoon thyme

1 oz butter
3 oz white bread-crumbs
1 egg
salt and pepper
pinch nutmeg

Pour boiling water over the two livers to blanch them, then chop finely, adding the herbs, seasoning, nutmeg, bread-crumbs and melted butter. Bind with the lightly beaten egg and stuff the duckling with the liver mixture. Truss the bird, baste well with hot fat, and place in a hot oven, 425° F (Gas 7). Cook for 30 minutes, basting twice. Then drain off the fat, pour the brown sauce (hot) into the baking tin and continue cooking until the duckling is tender, basting the bird frequently with the sauce.

Peel and section the orange, place it in a basin with some wine or stock, and heat it over a pan of hot water. When the bird is ready, place on a serving dish, strain a little of the sauce round the bird, and garnish with the hot orange. Pour the rest of the sauce in a sauce-boat to pass separately. (See Brown Sauce recipe below.)

SERVES 3–4

Brown Sauce
1 small carrot, thinly sliced
1 oz flour
1 onion, thinly sliced
1 pint good stock
1 oz dripping
salt and pepper

Melt the dripping and in it gently fry the onion and carrot until golden brown. Stir in the flour, lower the heat, fry very slowly until the flour too is brown. Then add the stock, bring to simmering point, season, and simmer for 25 minutes. Strain the stock before using. If the colour is not quite deep enough for your taste, you may add a little gravy browning or meat or vegetable extract to add depth of colour as well as an extra flavour.

PORTUGUESE DUCK

1 duck (about 5 lb)
1 apple, 1 slice onion, 2 celery
1 cup port
stalks
celery stalks or vine leaves *or*
salt and pepper

Wipe the duck inside and out with a damp cloth. Season the cavity with salt and pepper, and in it place some scrubbed celery stalks, or vine leaves or an apple, quartered but unpeeled, a slice of onion and 2 celery stalks. (Remove these items once the bird is cooked.) Truss the bird if required and then prick the skin on the fatty back layer and around legs and wings with a sharp fork. Do not dig the fork too deeply into the bird or the fat will tend to run into the bird instead of running out. Place the bird, breast side up, on a wire rack in a baking tin. Pour about $\frac{1}{2}$ cup of port into the tin, and place the tin in the oven, 350° F (Gas 4). Cook, allowing about 30 minutes per pound, basting frequently with the wine and the juices from the bird, adding more wine as required, or until you have used up the entire cupful. The skin of the bird should be brown and crisp by the time it is tender. Dish and serve with roast or French-fried potatoes and green peas. Strain the gravy from the dripping and wine and pass separately in a sauce-boat.

SERVES 3–4

CHINESE ROAST DUCK

1 duck (about 5 lb)	4 spring onions (optional)
2 tablespoons brandy or	salt
sherry	3 teaspoons Worcester sauce
1½ dessertspoons soy sauce	2 tablespoons honey
1 clove garlic, crushed	1 cup hot water

Mix together the brandy or sherry, soy sauce, crushed garlic, chopped spring onions, Worcester sauce and salt. Pour this mixture into the duck's cavity and rub well in. Seal the opening and wipe the duck dry on the outside. Mix together the honey and water and pour this over the duck a number of times (at least 8 times). Leave until dry and then repeat the process. The honey will give colour and crispness to the skin.

Meanwhile heat the oven to 375° F (Gas 5) and roast the duck breast upwards on a grid in a shallow roasting tin. Turn the bird in about 20 minutes when it has become a rich reddish brown and cook for a further 20 minutes. Brush with the drippings from time to time, turn the bird breast side uppermost again, and cook till tender and well browned. Place on a serving dish, reduce the gravy from the pan and serve it with the bird.

An alternative method is to omit the savoury mixture for the cavity and simply glaze the bird with the honey and warm water. (In this case reduce water to ¾ cup.) Leave it to stand for 2 to 3 hours so that the honey glaze will be absorbed, and then roast on a spit or rotisserie. Serve the duck cut into small pieces with the crisp skin cut into crackling strips.

SERVES 3–4

CANETON NANTAIS

1 duck (about 3 lb)	3 to 4 rashers streaky bacon
2 oz butter	quartered
4 medium onions, quartered	¾ pint stock
	8 oz packet peas

Pre-heat the oven at 375° F (Gas 5). Remove the giblets from the duckling and simmer in a little water to make the stock. Melt the butter in a roasting tin and cook the duck for 30 minutes. Remove the duck from the roasting tin and place in a deep casserole, add the onion, bacon and stock. Cover and cook for another 30 minutes. Add the peas to the casserole and continue cooking for a further 15 minutes or until the duck is tender. Serve on a large dish with the vegetables and stock spooned round.

SERVES 2

DUCK WITH PEACHES

1 duck (about 5 lb)	½ cup vermouth
1 tablespoon sugar	6 peaches
2 oz butter	salt and pepper
½ cup stock	

Peel, halve and stone the peaches. Sprinkle them with vermouth and set aside. Melt the butter in a roasting dish and brown the duck well in it all over, sprinkling it with sugar as you brown it. Pour in the stock, add seasoning. Cover with foil, and cook in the oven until tender. Remove the covering for the last 20 minutes of cooking to brown the breast. When cooked, place the duck on a heated serving dish and keep it hot. Spoon off the fat from the pan in which the duck has been cooked. Place in the remaining gravy the peach halves and the rest of the vermouth. Leave to simmer for 2 to 3 minutes, garnish with the peach halves and pour sauce over the bird.

SERVES 3–4

DUCK WITH RED CABBAGE

1 duck (about 5 lb)	½ pint red wine
1 medium red cabbage	2 tablespoons lemon juice
1 onion	½ teaspoon sugar
1½ oz butter	salt and pepper

Rub the duck with salt both inside and out. Roast in a moderate oven for 1 hour, then remove it from the pan and keep it hot, draining off the excess fat from the pan juices. Meanwhile shred the cabbage, sprinkle with salt and leave it to sweat about 15 minutes. Squeeze out this liquid and drain the cabbage thoroughly. Chop the onion and fry it until soft in the heated butter. Add the drained cabbage, stir thoroughly together and cook for 2 to 3 minutes, then add the wine, sugar, the seasoning and the lemon juice. Cover the pan and cook over a low heat for about 20 minutes. Now transfer the cabbage mixture to your roasting pan and place the duck on top of it. Cook the bird in the oven for about a further hour, or until it is tender.

SERVES 3–4

DUCK WITH APRICOTS

1 duck (3 to 4 lb)	3 level teaspoons cornflour
1 dessertspoon honey	1 teaspoon lemon juice
1 (15 oz) tin apricot halves	butter
3 tablespoons apricot brandy	

Prepare and roast the duck in a moderate oven, but after it has been cooking for about 50 minutes, remove it from the oven and prick it very lightly to allow surplus fat to run out. Now brush the bird with a little warm honey, so as to give it a crisp brown skin, and put it back in the oven to finish cooking.

Meanwhile, make the sauce. Strain the liquid from the apricots and to it add the juice of the lemon and enough water to make up a total quantity of just under ½ pint. Blend in the cornflour, pour into a saucepan and cook until the sauce is smooth, thick and clear. Check the flavour and add a little sugar or honey if it is not sweet enough. Stir in a spoonful of butter to impart shine to the sauce. Place the apricot halves in the sauce, heat through for a few moments, and then stir in the apricot brandy. Be careful not to let the sauce boil. Now remove the bird from the oven, place it on a heated serving dish, either whole or carved into joints. Top with the sauce and apricots, and garnish with a few sprigs of watercress.

SERVES 2–3

DUCK WITH CHERRIES

1 duck (4½ to 5 lb)	2 level tablespoons flour
1 (16 oz) tin cherries	1 teaspoon sugar
3 tablespoons vermouth	1 oz fat
8 oz streaky bacon rashers	

Place the fat in a roasting pan and pre-heat the oven to 400° F (Gas 6). Stuff the duck with the forcemeat of your choice, retruss and place it in the roasting pan. Tip the cherries into a bowl and stir in the vermouth. Wet the duck all over with the mixture, then cover the breast with about 4 bacon rashers. Sprinkle flour and sugar in the pan and bake for 10 minutes. Now reduce the heat to 325° F (Gas 3) and cook for a further 1½ hours or until the bird is tender.

Meanwhile boil the giblets in about ½ pint water for 30 minutes and make bacon rolls with the remaining streaky bacon by removing their rinds and rolling them up and baking on a fireproof plate in the oven for about ¼ hour. When the duck is ready, place on a heated serving dish. Spoon off as much of the fat from the pan as possible. Pour the giblet broth and the cherry and vermouth syrup into the pan, add salt and pepper and cook until the sauce is smooth and thick. Garnish the bird with cherries and bacon rolls and pour the sauce around the dish.

SERVES 3–4

SPICED MALAY DUCK

1 duck (about 3 lb)
1 cup plus 3 tablespoons
thick coconut milk (see below)
1 tablespoon vinegar

½ tablespoon salt
1 dessertspoon sugar
2 hard-boiled eggs

For the paste
2½ tablespoons anise seeds
½ tablespoon cumin seeds
5 tablespoons coriander seeds
1 teaspoon turmeric

2 inches ginger root
¼ lb shallots
2 clove garlic

Onion mixture
2 oz shallots
2 fresh chillies, seeded (a
quarter green pepper may be
used instead for a milder
flavour)

2 medium onions

Grind together and mix to a thick paste the ingredients for the paste and set aside a dessertspoon of this mixture. Slice the onion mixture ingredients finely. Now finely chop the heart, liver and gizzard of the bird and mix them with the cup of coconut milk, the sliced onion mixture, the ground spice mixture, the vinegar, salt and sugar. Cook this mixture over a medium heat for about 15 minutes and then stuff it into the vent end of the duck, with the hard-boiled eggs (whole). Now mix the three tablespoons of coconut milk with the reserved dessertspoon of ground spices and smear this over the bird. Grill the duck on a barbecue, or on a rotisserie, over direct heat or under a grill, placing it about 4 inches from the heat. Turn the bird frequently, dabbing it with the spicy paste until it forms a coating. This is rather a slow method of cooking duck, but the result is delicious.

To make coconut milk
Pour tepid water (about ½ to ¾ cup per nut) on to coarsely grated fresh coconut flesh or dessicated coconut. Leave 10 minutes, then squeeze well and strain through a fine nylon sieve.

SERVES 2–3

PEKING DUCK

1 duckling (about 5 lb)   boiling water

For the sauce
1 cup soy sauce   good pinch pepper
½ cup sherry   3 spring onions, finely
6 dessertspoons brown sugar   chopped
1 dessertspoon salt   2 cloves garlic, crushed

This is a traditional Chinese dish, which calls for a double cooking method of simmering and deep frying, to produce a bird which is crisp on the outside and tender on the inside. It does, however, have to be spread over two days.

First day. Mix the ingredients for the sauce, and place the sauce together with the duck in a deep vessel. Pour on enough boiling water almost to cover the bird, then cover it tightly with a lid or foil and simmer it until almost done, about 60 minutes. Lift the duck from the liquid and hang it to dry overnight. This can be done by tying the duck by the neck to the top rack in the oven, removing all other racks, and putting a foil-lined dish underneath. Before completing the dish next day, be sure that the duck is thoroughly dry or the dish will not be successful.

When ready to prepare the duck for the meal, heat about three inches of oil to 375° F (Gas 5) and brown the duck on all sides, which will only take a very few minutes. Carve and serve.

In China, Peking Duck is eaten wrapped in small, thin pancakes, together with a plum sauce, spring onions and cucumber.

SERVES 3–4

DUCK IN BEER

1 duck (about 5 lb)   bouquet garni (2 sprigs
3 oz butter   parsley, 1 sprig each thyme,
1 onion, finely chopped   marjoram, 1 bay leaf)
½ pint beer   salt and pepper
1 lb seedless grapes

Melt the butter in a casserole and in it brown the onion and the duck. When the duck is brown on all sides, pour in the beer,

add the bouquet garni and seasoning. Cover and cook until
tender, basting with the juices from time to time. Test for
tenderness after about an hour. When the duck is done, take
it from the pan and keep it hot. Remove the bouquet garni from
the pan juices, strain off as much fat as possible, then add the
grapes and simmer them in the gravy for a few moments.
Meanwhile cut the duck into portions. Arrange on the serving-
dish, and when the sauce is ready, pour it and the grapes over
the portions and serve.

SERVES 3–4

BRAISED DUCKLING

1 duckling (about 5 lb)	1½ oz flour
a little hot fat	1 pint stock
2 onions	2 sage leaves
2 oz butter	sprig of thyme

Baste the trussed duck with hot fat and place to cook in a hot
oven, 425° F (Gas 7) until well browned. Baste the bird every
few minutes. Meanwhile, slice the onions finely, and fry them
in the butter until golden brown. Remove from the fat and stir
into it the flour, cooking until that too is brown. Remove the
duck from the oven, place in a large saucepan, pour stock over
it almost to cover the bird, then add the fried onions, seasoning
and herbs, and cover with a closely-fitting lid. Simmer gently
until tender (45 to 60 minutes). When the duck is cooked, strain
the sauce from the pan, and stir about ¾ of a pint of it into your
brown roux. Bring to the boil, stirring, and cook for 5 minutes.
Taste for seasoning and adjust as necessary. Serve the duck
with the gravy and with buttered green peas.

SERVES 3–4

BRAISED DUCKLING AND PINEAPPLE

1 duckling (about 5 lb)	½ pint brown sauce (see
1 small (7½ oz) tin pineapple	page 171)
chunks	1 teaspoon tomato ketchup
½ pint inexpensive white wine	a little dripping

Drain the pineapple, place the chunks in the wine and leave to soak for several hours. When ready to cook the dish, place the duck in dripping in the oven for about 40 minutes (325° F, Gas 3), and then drain off all the fat. Drain the pineapple, mix the liquid with the brown sauce and tomato ketchup, and pour it over the duck. Cover the dish with a closely-fitting lid or aluminium foil and put it back in the oven for a further hour, at 375° F (Gas 5). Just before you are ready to serve, place the pineapple pieces in a saucepan to heat through. Put the duck on a hot dish and garnish with the pineapple, then pour the sauce over the bird, either whole or already carved.

SERVES 3–4

LUXURY DUCK A L'ORANGE

1 tender duckling, ready prepared (5 to 6 lb)
6 tablespoons corn oil
¼ pint Cointreau
1 tablespoon sugar
1 tablespoon white wine vinegar
5 oranges
2 tablespoons cranberry sauce
¼ pint beef stock
watercress for garnish
salt and pepper

Joint the duck. Heat the corn oil in a casserole and sauté the duck until evenly browned. Reduce the heat, cover and simmer gently until tender, turning from time to time. Add two-thirds of the Cointreau and simmer for 5 minutes. Remove the duck and keep hot. Add the vinegar, sugar, juice of 1 orange, cranberry sauce and beef stock. Bring to the boil, stirring all the time. Reduce the heat and simmer gently for 10 minutes. Skim the fat from the surface and strain the sauce. Season according to taste and add remaining Cointreau. Peel and segment the remaining oranges. Place half of them in the sauce and bring to the boil. Place duck on a serving-dish, pour a little sauce around the duck. Garnish with remaining orange segments and watercress. Serve the remaining sauce separately.

SERVES 4

DUCKLING WITH OLIVES

1 duckling (about 5 lb)   3 dozen olives
1 pint beef stock   salt and pepper
2 onions

Joint the duck, season and place in a casserole. Chop the onions,
the duck's liver, gizzard and heart and a dozen stoned olives.
Place this mixture on the joints and cover with the hot stock.
Simmer for 1 hour to 1¼ hours, gently, until the duck is tender.
Just before you are ready to serve, place the remaining olives
in the casserole for a few minutes. When the duck is cooked,
lift the pieces on to a hot serving-dish and pour over it the sauce,
garnished with the olives.

SERVES 3–4

CHINESE SAVOURY DUCK

1 duck (about 3 lb)   3 dessertspoons frying oil
2 cups water   1 medium onion
1 dessertspoon cornflour   1 clove garlic
2 dessertspoons water   1 or 2 thin slices ginger

For sauce
1 cup soy sauce   2 dessertspoons brown sugar
2 dessertspoons dry sherry   1 scant teaspoon salt

Heat the oil in a deep frying-pan to about 350° F (Gas 4).
Quickly fry the duck cut into 6 or 8 pieces until golden brown.
Drain off the excess oil, then add the onions, garlic and ginger
and fry with the duck for a further 2 minutes. Meanwhile, mix
the sauce ingredients together and add the sauce to the duck
in the pan. Mix well, then pour over two cups water and bring
to the boil. Cover the pan and leave to simmer gently for about
2 hours. Just before you are ready to serve, add the cornflour
moistened with 2 dessertspoons of water, to thicken the sauce.
Stir and cook for a further 2 minutes before serving.

SERVES 2

SAVOURY DUCK WITH CHESTNUTS

1 duck (3 lb)   condiments and sauce as for
2 cups water   Chinese Savoury Duck
1 lb chestnuts   (page 180)

Place the chestnuts in boiling water in a deep pan and boil for
30 minutes. Cool and shell the chestnuts. Meanwhile cook the
duck as for Savoury Duck (page 180), and simmer for 1½ hours,
covered. Now add the chestnuts and cook, covered, for a
further 30 minutes on a low heat.

SERVES 2

DUCK WITH YOUNG TURNIPS

1 duckling (about 5 lb)   ½ cup stock (for a touch of
2 oz butter   luxury, substitute dry white
1 lb young turnips   wine, or a mixture of stock
pinch thyme   and wine)
2 teaspoons chopped parsley   salt and pepper
1 small onion, finely chopped

Melt half the butter in a pan and in it brown the duck, cut into
joints together with the onion. Next add the wine or stock,
seasonings and herbs, cover and cook on a low gas for 50 to
60 minutes. Meanwhile, boil the turnips in salted water until
just tender, then drain and sauté them lightly in the remaining
butter, making sure that they do not brown. The turnips can
then either be added to the pan and cooked for a few minutes
with the duckling, or they can be piled onto a serving-dish,
sprinkled with chopped parsley and with the duckling joints
arranged around them, and the sauce from the casserole poured
over.

SERVES 3–4

CASSOULET OF DUCK

1 duck (about 4 lb)   1 large can tomatoes
3 onions   (1 lb 12 oz)
1 lb carrots   2 cloves garlic, crushed

¼ teaspoon mixed herbs   salt and pepper
1 teaspoon finely grated
orange rind

Wipe the duck with a clean, damp cloth, and cut into 8 joints. Peel and chop the onions and carrots and place in a large casserole, with the tomatoes, garlic, herbs, orange rind and seasoning. Place the duck joints, skin side uppermost, on top of these ingredients, cover with a lid or foil and bake at 325° F (Gas 3) for 2 hours. Take the lid off for the last 20 minutes of cooking time and raise the heat to 400° F (Gas 6) in order to brown the duck. Before serving, skim off as much of the excess fat as possible. This makes a quantity sufficient for at least 4 servings.

CASSEROLED DUCK WITH RICE

1 duck (about 5 lb)   ½ pint stock
2 onions, chopped   a little fat
3 carrots, sliced   ¼ lb Portuguese sausage
1 tablespoon chopped parsley   salt and pepper
8 oz long grain rice

Joint the duck and place it together with the onions, carrots, parsley and seasoning, in an ovenproof casserole, Pour on the stock, cover, and cook for about 1½ hours at 350° F (Gas 4). Next drain off the stock, replace the casserole in the warm oven. Make up the stock to ¾ pint using water or other stock, and place it in a pan together with the rice. Bring to the boil, cover, simmer for about 15 minutes, or until the rice is tender and the liquid has been absorbed. Take care not to let the mixture get too dry, adding a little more liquid if necessary

Meanwhile slice the sausage and fry in a little hot fat until well brown. Place half the rice on a serving dish, arrange on it the duckling joints, cover with the remaining rice and garnish with the sausage pieces.

SERVES 3–4

FLORENTINE DUCK

1 young duckling, jointed
(about 5 lb)
1 lb tomatoes, chopped
¼ pint red wine
½ teaspoon mixed herbs

1 oz butter
2 oz papper-delle (flat
macaroni)
salt and pepper

Place the tomatoes in a saucepan with the butter and cook till soft. Now add the duck, the wine, herbs and seasonings. Cover and simmer for 1¼ hours, then add the papper-delle and cook gently for a further 15 minutes or until the papper-delle is soft.

SERVES 3–4

CASSEROLED DUCK WITH CURAÇAO SAUCE

1 duck (4 to 4½ lb)
2½ level tablespoons flour
1 level teaspoon celery salt
2 onions, chopped
6 oz mushrooms
½ cup water

1 tablespoon soy sauce
3 tablespoons curaçao liqueur
½ teaspoon dried basil
3 oranges
a little sugar
salt and pepper

Place the flour, celery salt and a little pepper in a paper bag. Shake well, and in this seasoned flour toss the duck, cut into pieces. Shake well to coat evenly and then place the duck joints in a deep casserole. Sprinkle with the chopped onions and any flour remaining in the bag. Peel the mushrooms, slice them and add to the casserole. Mix the water, soy sauce, curaçao and one level teaspoon of salt together and pour this over the duck. Sprinkle with the dried basil, cover and bake for 1½ to 2 hours, until the joints are very tender. Cook at 325° F (Gas 3), but if the gravy is boiling too fast after the first half-hour, reduce the heat.

Meanwhile, peel and slice the oranges, place them on a flat oven-proof dish and sprinkle with the sugar. Heat through in the oven for about 10 minutes before the dish is ready, and use the orange slices to garnish the finished dish, together with a few sprigs of parsley. This quantity should make about 6 servings. You can, if you wish, substitute 4 tablespoons of fresh orange juice and 1 level tablespoon of sugar in place of the curaçao.

SALMI OF DUCK

1 duck (about 5 lb)
4 oz button mushrooms
8 oz larger mushrooms
1 glass port

few fresh apricots or peaches
or tinned pineapple rings
bottled Cumberland sauce

Espagnole sauce
2 onions, chopped
1 large carrot, chopped
2 oz lean bacon, chopped
2 oz butter
1 heaped tablespoon flour

8 oz tomatoes, fresh or
canned
1 glass white wine
1½ pints stock
bouquet garni (parsley,
thyme, bay leaf)

Prepare the duck for roasting, but do not stuff. Baste with hot fat and place in a hot oven, 400° F (Gas 6), allowing about 15 minutes per pound, and cook until the skin is crisp and brown but the meat still pink and underdone. Remove the bird from the oven, cool it until it can be handled, cut into serving pieces, making two pieces of each leg and cutting the breast into four.

Espagnole sauce
While the bird is cooking make the Espagnole sauce by frying the onions, carrot and bacon in the butter until they are a rich brown. Sprinkle in the flour, continue frying until that too has cooked to a golden brown. Now add the tomatoes, the wine and stock. Bring to the boil, stirring constantly. Finally add the bouquet garni, and simmer uncovered for an hour, stirring occasionally to prevent sticking. Strain the sauce into a clean pan, pressing the mixture in the strainer to squeeze as much liquid as possible. Simmer again for about 20 minutes, and the sauce is now ready to use.

Meanwhile, boil the button mushrooms in salted water for 5 minutes, strain and reserve for garnish. Stir the glass of port into the Espagnole sauce, reheat and add Cumberland sauce, a dessertspoon at a time, until you have got as much of an orangey flavour as you want. If you have no Cumberland sauce, then use orange juice and grated rind. Put the larger mushrooms in a casserole and on top of them the pieces of duck. Check the flavouring of the sauce and add salt and pepper if necessary, then pour the sauce over the duck, cover and cook slowly in the oven for ¾ hour or until tender. Serve on to a warm dish, garnish with the button mushrooms and the fruit (apricots peaches or pineapple), heated through.

SERVES 3–4

COLD OR LEFT-OVER DUCK

Duck being less fleshy than chicken in proportion to its size, there is not usually much to use up as 'left-overs'. However, if you have some remains from a cooked bird, you will find plenty of ideas among the Chicken Left-overs section which can be used. Similarly, many of the cold dishes and salad ideas are equally suitable for cold duck, if you want to cook your bird in advance for a cold meal.

SMALL GAME
BIRDS

PHEASANT

In season October to February
Although the cock bird is more beautiful to look at, country-men declare that the hen bird is better to eat, especially cold.

In a young bird, the first wing-tip feather is pointed; in an older bird, it is rounded. If the upper part of the beak is pliable, you may be sure that you have a young bird.

An average-sized pheasant makes four servings, but before cooking it needs to be well hung, otherwise the flesh will be tasteless and dry. Hang the bird, unplucked, in a good current of air, for at least three days. In warm or muggy weather, this should be sufficient for the putrefaction process to have begun, but if the weather is cold, longer time should be allowed. It is, of course, important to keep flies away, and a thorough sprinkling of the feathers with pepper helps to do so. Individual tastes vary as to how 'high' a bird should be before it is ready for cooking. Unless you wish to have a very gamey flavour, the bird will be ready for plucking when the tail feathers pull out easily. If, when you come to cook the bird, you find it has become rather too 'high' for your liking, wash the bird, when plucked, in salted water to which vinegar has been added, then rinse thoroughly. Pluck, draw, truss and singe the bird, as for chicken.

ROAST PHEASANT

1 pheasant
butter
strips fat bacon

flour
salt and pepper

Tie strips of fat bacon across the breast of the seasoned bird, and place a piece of butter in the cavity. Pour melted butter over the bird and roast in a pre-heated hot oven (450° F, Gas 8) for about 10 minutes, then reduce the heat to 400° F (Gas 6). Cook for about a further 45 minutes, or until tender, but baste frequently with the butter during cooking. About 15 minutes before cooking is completed, remove the bacon from the breast, dredge with flour, baste again and complete cooking. Dish the bird on to a hot dish, remove the trussing strings and serve with the bread sauce, fried or oven-roasted bread-crumbs and thin gravy.

As a variation of the above, place about 4 ounces rump steak in the bird's cavity before cooking. This can be reserved and eaten cold for another meal. For this method, dripping can replace butter for roasting fat.

Here are some other recipes for roasting pheasant, giving a variety of flavourings.

FRENCH ROAST PHEASANT

1 pheasant	1 tablespoon cream cheese
2 oz belly of pork	1 tablespoon double cream
6 walnuts, coarsely chopped	butter
2 dozen seedless grapes	salt and pepper
strips of fat bacon	

Chop the liver, mince the belly of pork. Mix together, then add the cheese, walnuts, cream and grapes. Season, and place this stuffing in the bird's cavity, stitching up the opening. Truss the bird, brush with butter, tie fat bacon strips over the breast, season, and roast at 400° F (Gas 6) for about 45 to 50 minutes or until tender. Use the remaining giblets to make a gravy.

CHESTNUT-STUFFED PHEASANT

fat bacon strips	4 oz white bread-crumbs
1 pheasant	4 chipolata sausages
1 lb chestnuts	1 tablespoon chopped parsley

2 oz celery, chopped
1 teaspoon salt
⅛ teaspoon pepper

½ cup melted butter
2 tablespoons cream

Cook, shell, skin and sieve the chestnuts, then mix with the chipolata sausages, finely chopped, the crumbs, parsley, celery, seasonings, butter and cream. Prepare the pheasant in the usual way, stuff with the above mixture, tie fat bacon pieces across the breast and roast as in previous recipe.

SAUSAGE-AND-LIVER-STUFFED PHEASANT

1 pheasant
fat bacon strips
8 oz sausage meat
3 chicken livers
1 egg yolk
1 tablespoon cream
1 glass sherry

1 dessertspoon tomato purée
nutmeg
½ teaspoon chopped parsley
butter
a little stock
salt and pepper

Mix together the sausage meat, the chicken livers (chopped) and parsley. Season with salt and pepper and bind to a stiff mixture with the beaten egg yolk and cream. Prepare the bird as usual, stuff with the mixture and tie fat bacon strips across the breast. Baste with melted butter and roast at 400° F (Gas 6) for 15 minutes. Lower the heat to 375° F (Gas 5) for 10 minutes longer, then pour into the pan the wine, tomato purée and a dash of nutmeg, together with a little stock made from the bird's giblets. Continue roasting the bird until tender, basting frequently with the sauce in the pan, and use this sauce to pour over the bird when it is ready for serving.

ITALIAN PHEASANT WITH CREAM

1 pheasant
fat bacon strips
2 oz butter
1 small onion

½ pint double cream
1 tablespoon lemon juice
salt and pepper

Tie the bacon strips across the breast of the seasoned pheasant, baste with melted butter and cook very slowly for about 2 hours.

Remove the bacon for the last 30 minutes, pour the cream over the bird, and baste frequently. When the pheasant is ready for serving add the lemon juice to the gravy remaining in the pan, mix well, and serve with the bird.

PHEASANT IN WINE SAUCE

1 pheasant	1 cup stock
fat bacon strips	$\frac{1}{2}$ cup red wine
salt and pepper	$\frac{1}{4}$ teaspoon meat extract
2 oz butter	

Prepare and roast the pheasant as on page 189, until tender, Remove the bird to a serving dish, pour off the fat carefully from the pan, then add the wine, stock (made from bird giblets if possible) and meat extract. Bring slowly to the boil, stirring vigorously to incorporate all the goodness from the pan, then pour a little of the sauce over the bird, serving the remainder in a sauce-boat.

BRANDIED PHEASANT

1 pheasant	1 teaspoon brandy
8 oz cooked fresh pork	1 sharp apple
1 chicken liver	2 strips fat bacon
1 pheasant liver	1 teaspoon Madeira
pinch thyme	$\frac{1}{2}$ cup stock
pinch rosemary	salt and pepper

Mince the pork, lean and fat, together with the chicken and pheasant livers, add thyme and rosemary, stir in the brandy and the apple previously peeled and diced. Next add the seasoning and stuff the bird with this mixture. Truss it and tie the bacon strips over the breast. Roast in a 350° F (Gas 4) oven for about an hour or until brown and tender, basting frequently with the pan juices. When the bird is cooked, remove it to a warm serving dish. Discard the bacon. Into the roasting pan put a $\frac{1}{2}$ cup of good stock. Stir the pan thoroughly to incoporate all the juices from the bird and then pour the sauce into a small sauce-pan. Skim the fat from the surface, stir in the Madeira, reheat and serve this sauce with the bird.

DEVILLED PHEASANT

1 pheasant	Diable
½ pint double cream	½ cup milk
½ teaspoon mustard	8 oz mushrooms
½ teaspoon Worcester sauce	butter
½ teaspoon Escoffier's Sauce	salt and pepper

Roast the pheasant in the usual manner. Meanwhile cook the mushrooms in butter in readiness for when the bird is cooked. Mix the cream, milk, mustard, sauces together and season with salt and pepper. When the bird is tender cut it into pieces, place on an earthenware dish and pour the cream sauce over it. Put it back in the oven but make sure that it does not boil. Serve with the mushrooms.

CASSEROLE OF PHEASANT WITH CHESTNUTS

1 tablespoon corn oil	1 teaspoon red wine vinegar
1 pheasant	bouquet garni
8 oz chestnuts, peeled	¾ oz cornflour
8 oz button onions	1 chicken stock cube dissolved
grated rind and juice of ½	in ¾ pint of boiling water
orange	2 tablespoons chopped
1 dessertspoon cranberry	parsley
sauce	salt and pepper

Heat the corn oil in a casserole and slowly brown the pheasant. Remove from the pan. Sauté the chestnuts and onions until browned. Remove from the pan, add the cornflour. Stir in the chicken stock, grated rind and juice from orange, cranberry sauce, red wine vinegar, bouquet garni and seasoning. Bring to the boil, stirring all the time. Add the pheasant, chestnuts and onions. Cover and cook in a slow oven, 325° F (gas 3) for 1½ to 2 hours. When cooked, joint the pheasant and place on a clean serving dish with chestnuts and onions. Remove the bouquet garni from the sauce. Adjust the seasoning if necessary. Pour over the pheasant and sprinkle with chopped parsley.

CASSEROLLED PHEASANT

1 pheasant	½ pint chicken stock
4 oz mushrooms	¼ pint orange juice
1 oz butter	2 wine glasses white wine
1 tablespoon oil	2 oz flour
1 orange	salt and pepper

Melt the oil and butter in a pan and fry the pheasant, previously plucked, drawn and jointed, on each side. When the joints are well brown, lift from the pan into an ovenproof casserole. Fry the mushrooms for a few minutes, add them to the casserole. Season. Stir the flour into the fat in the pan, cook for 2 minutes, remove from the heat, and gradually add the stock, wine and orange juice. Bring to the boil, stirring, and when it thickens pour it into the casserole. Place the dish in the middle of the oven and cook until the pheasant is tender. Skin the orange, remove the pith so that only the outer skin remains, and cut this into thin strips. Simmer the orange strips in water until soft, then when the casserole is ready, sprinkle them over the bird portions, and garnish with orange segments.

GRILLED PHEASANT

1 pheasant	4 oz mushrooms
2 oz butter	2 tomatoes
1 egg	watercress
bread-crumbs	salt and pepper

Melt the butter in a pan and in it place the bird, jointed, and season. Fry until the pieces are lightly browned, then remove from the pan and press them between two plates until quite cold. Next coat the pieces with egg and bread-crumbs, place under a grill for a few minutes until the coating has set, then brush with melted butter and cook, turning frequently, for about 25 to 30 minutes. Serve, garnished with grilled mushrooms, tomatoes and sprigs of watercress.

BRAISED PHEASANT

1 pheasant	1 small onion
1 thin slice salt pork	2 teaspoons flour
1 tangerine	$\frac{1}{4}$ cup Madeira
1 oz lard or cooking fat	$\frac{1}{2}$ teaspoon salt
1 dozen mushrooms	a little freshly-ground pepper
1 oz butter	1 sprig fresh fennel (optional)

Prepare the pheasant for cooking, pre-heat the oven to 400°F (Gas 6). Flatten the slice of pork and insert it under the skin of the breast flesh. Into the body cavity place the pheasant's liver and the tangerine (peeled), then close the cavity by stitching tightly. Truss the pheasant and brown it in the lard melted in a heavy pan. Baste and turn frequently until the bird is golden all over and then transfer it to a casserole. In the fat fry the mushrooms, using the caps only, for a few moments, and then place them over the pheasant in the casserole. In a saucepan melt the butter and in it cook the onion, minced or very finely chopped, and the flour. Cook but do not allow this onion to brown. When soft, gradually stir in the Madeira, salt and pepper and pour the sauce over the bird. Add a sprig of fennel if available, then cover the casserole and cook for 30 to 40 minutes until the pheasant is tender.

GUINEA FOWL

Guinea fowl has grey plumage with white spots and is generally a little larger than pheasant. Although available all the year round, it is at its prime best from February to June. Choose a bird with a plump breast and smooth-skinned feet, but be sure not to cook it too soon after it has been killed.

A guinea fowl is prepared in exactly the same way as chicken and may be cooked similarly too, especially casseroling and stewing. However, this bird lacks fat so it is important to make sure that, when roasting, the flesh does not dry out in cooking. It should be covered with bacon strips or fat bacon and basted frequently or, alternatively, wrapped in aluminium foil.

ROAST GUINEA FOWL

1 guinea fowl	2 oz butter
2 to 4 slices fat bacon	salt and pepper

Beat the salt and pepper into the butter and place it in the cavity of the prepared bird. Truss. Lay the slices of bacon over the breast and place in a baking tin. Baste with a little melted butter. Roast in a fairly hot oven, 375° F (Gas 5), for 1 to 1½ hours depending on size. Baste frequently. When the bird is almost ready, dredge the breast with flour, baste again and finish cooking. Serve with browned crumbs and bread-sauce.

ROAST GUINEA FOWL WITH GRAPES

1 guinea fowl	2 tablespoons flour
3 oz softened butter	½ lb green grapes
sprig parsley	½ glass sherry
4 to 5 rashers fat bacon	bouquet garni
giblet stock	salt and pepper

Make some stock with water, the giblets and the bouquet garni. Season with a little pepper and salt. Put half butter and parsley sprig inside the bird cavity. Spread the remaining butter thickly over the bird and cover the breast with the bacon. Roast in a pre-heated oven at 400° F (Gas 6) until golden brown and tender (about an hour). Baste frequently during this cooking time.

When the bird is cooked, remove it to a serving dish. Pour the fat carefully off the roasting tin leaving just a thin layer on the bottom. To this add sufficient flour to absorb the fat. Stirring continuously and scraping all the residue from the bottom of the pan, fry over the heat to make a roux. When this has become

a good colour, stir in about ¼ pint giblet stock and add the
sherry. Now add the green grapes, previously skinned and
seeded, and cook this sauce gently for about 10 minutes. Test for
seasoning. Add salt and pepper and, if liked, a squeeze of lemon
juice. Strain the gravy into a previously heated sauceboat and
garnish the serving-dish with the grapes.

BRAISED GUINEA FOWL A L'ORANGE

1 guinea fowl	stock
1 oz butter	1 teaspoon cornflour
½ carrot	orange liqueur (orange
1 medium onion	curaçao)
1 tablespoon diced bacon	salt and pepper
2 bouquets garnis	

Make stock from the wing tips, neck and giblets of the bird,
together with one slice taken from the onion, one of the
bouquets garnis, salt and pepper. Melt one tablespoon of the
butter in a heavy pan, and in this brown the prepared and trussed
guinea fowl on all sides. Meanwhile, in a casserole big enough
to take the bird, melt the other tablespoon of butter and in it
sauté slowly the half carrot, sliced, and the remainder of the
onion, chopped, together with the diced bacon. Add salt,
pepper and the remaining bouquet garni.

When the vegetables are lightly browned, place the guinea
fowl in the casserole and over it pour 2 tablespoons of the orange
liqueur. Set it aflame and when the flames have died, add one
cup of hot stock. Cover the casserole, and cook the bird at 350° F
(Gas 4) for about an hour or until tender. For the last 10 minutes
of cooking time, remove the lid in order to brown the bird.
When done, place it on a hot serving dish and keep it warm.
Skim the fat from the juices, strain them through a fine sieve.
Force the vegetables through the sieve, or blend in an electric
blender. Dissolve the cornflour in a little cold stock, add to the
gravy and sieved vegetables and reheat, stirring until the sauce
thickens. When cooked, stir in 2 teaspoons of the orange liqueur.
Cut the bird into 4 portions. Garnish with a little chopped parsley and hand the sauce separately in a hot sauce-boat.

GROUSE

In season 12 August to 10 December
A young bird will have soft downy feathers on its breast, and
when you hold it by the lower mandible between your finger and
thumb, moving it gently up and down, the mandible should
bend or break. Older grouse are perfectly usable but they
should be casseroled and not roasted or grilled.

Hang the birds by their legs for at least three days, preferably
five or six, according to the weather. Then pluck and draw them
as for pheasant. The plucking is a more delicate operation than
with pheasant and should be done with the greatest possible
care so as not to tear the skin.

ROAST GROUSE
1 or more birds

For each bird

1 oz butter *or* 4 oz rump steak	1 slice toast
1 rasher bacon	salt and pepper
flour	

Into each bird insert either 1 ounce butter or a piece of rump
steak seasoned with salt and pepper. (The steak can be used for
a cold meat and salad dish on another occasion.) Cover the
breast of the bird with bacon and roast at 375° F to 400° F
(Gas 5–6) until tender (about 30 minutes) in the centre of the
oven. Baste frequently. When the bird has been cooking for
about 20 minutes remove the bacon, dredge the breast with
flour and return it to the oven on a slice of toast. During the
rest of the cooking time, the bread will absorb the liquid which
drips from the bird. Serve on the toast on which it was roasted
with bread sauce, fried or oven-baked crumbs and thin gravy.

CASEROLED GROUSE

1 grouse (or more)	freshly-ground black pepper
2 tablespoons flour	dry draught cider
2 tablespoons olive oil	pinch of thyme
1 oz butter	1 clove garlic, finely chopped
1 onion	4 oz mushrooms

Using a knife and shears, cut the birds in half lengthwise. Place the onion, finely sliced, in a large bowl. Place on it the pieces of grouse, the pepper, some salt and cover with the cider. Leave the grouse to marinate overnight.

Next day, lift the grouse from the marinade, dry each piece, roll it in flour and fry in the olive oil and butter, mixed and melted in a casserole just large enough to take the bird or birds. Pour the marinade into the casserole, add the garlic, the mushrooms, a pinch of pepper and a sprinkling of thyme. If the bird or birds are still not covered, add sufficient water, then place the casserole in the oven, bring it to the boil, and then simmer until the meat leaves the bones easily (1¼ hours approximately). Serve with usual vegetables.

BANANA-STUFFED GROUSE

1 or more grouse	1 level teaspoon salt
2 bananas per bird	10 drops lemon juice
1 level teaspoon black pepper	

Skin the bananas, mash them and mix with the pepper, salt and lemon juice. Stuff this mixture into the grouse cavity and roast in the usual way (see page 198).

CASEROLED GROUSE AND SAUSAGE

2 grouse	1 small white cabbage
4 rashers streaky bacon	¼ pint dry red wine
4 dessertspoons flour	½ pint stock
2 oz butter or lard	4 smoked sausages
1 onion	black pepper
4 oz pickled belly of pork	salt

This recipe is excellent for older birds and makes a succulent meal.

Trim the rind and gristle from the bacon, and cover the breasts of the prepared birds. Truss them and roll in the flour, shaking off any surplus. Melt the butter or lard in a pan and in it brown the birds all over. Remove them from the pan, and in the remaining fat fry the onion (sliced) and the pickled pork (diced) until it is just lightly brown in colour.

Meanwhile shred the cabbage, discarding the stalk, and cook it for 5 minutes in boiling, salted water. Drain and put half the cabbage in the bottom of a casserole and add to it the fried pork and onion. Place the birds on top, pack in the remaining cabbage, season with pepper, then pour in the wine and stock, cover and cook either over a low heat on top of the stove, or in a moderate oven 325° F (Gas 3) for about 1½ hours or until tender. After the casserole has been cooking for about 45 minutes, add the smoked sausages, and put in a little extra liquid if required. Serve with boiled or baked potatoes. Do not use very much salt to season because the sausages are in themselves rather salty.

GROUSE PUDDING

1 grouse	4 oz suet
1 lb stewing steak	1 teaspoon baking powder
1 oz flour	cold water
½ pint stock	salt and pepper
8 oz plain flour	

First make the suet pastry. If using butcher's suet, chop it finely with a little flour; sift the flour, salt and baking powder together, mix in the suet and add enough cold water to make a firm dough.

Cut the steak and the flesh from the bird into small pieces and dip them in seasoned flour. Line a greased basin with two-thirds of your suet pastry, put into it the meat and half the stock. Make a lid with the remaining pastry, cover the basin and make a hole in the centre. Cover with a grease-proof paper and steam for 4 or more hours, pouring in the remaining stock, previously heated, at the half time mark.

An old bird can be used for this recipe. It will depend on the age and toughness of the bird as to how long you leave it to cook. You can if you wish add a sliced onion or a few mushrooms to the contents of the pudding.

BRAISED GROUSE

1 brace grouse	1 tablespoon cornflour
2 carrots, sliced	1 tablespoon sherry
2 onions, sliced	½ teaspoon soy sauce
1 small turnip, sliced	1 tablespoon jellied cranberry
bouquet garni	sauce
1 chicken stock cube	salt and pepper
¾ pint boiling water	

Prepare the grouse as for roasting. Place vegetables in the base of the casserole with bouquet garni. Dissolve the stock cube in boiling water. Put grouse on top and pour over the stock. Cover and cook in an oven at 350° F (Gas 4) for 1½ hours, basting occasionally with the stock. Remove the lid for the last ½ hour to brown the birds. Remove to a hot serving dish, strain the liquid from casserole and arrange the vegetables around the birds. Blend the stock with the cornflour. Pour into a pan and bring to the boil, stirring. Add sherry, soy sauce, cranberry jelly and season to taste. Reheat and pour over the grouse.

GROUSE PIE

Whole roast grouse can be bought in large tins and one of these used with pork fillet can make a large, party-sized pie, sufficient for eight or more servings.

1 tin whole roast grouse	salt and pepper
¾ lb pork fillet	

For the pastry

1½ lb plain flour	2 level teaspoons salt
7½ oz English lard	a little beaten egg for glazing
⅛ pint water	3 hard-boiled eggs

P.G.C.—10

To make this pie you will need a raised pie mould, about 8 inches long and $3\frac{1}{2}$ inches wide at the maximum. Open the tin of grouse, heat it to melt the jelly, remove all the bones and set the jelly on one side for use next day. Cut the pork fillets into one inch cubes and dust lightly with salt and pepper. Shell the hard-boiled eggs.

To make the pastry, sift the flour and salt into a bowl, put the lard and water into a saucepan, melt the lard over a low heat, bring it to the boil, and then pour it immediately into the flour mixing with a knife. Knead the dough by hand until it is quite smooth. Cut off a quarter of the pastry for the lid and set on one side in a warm place. Clip the halves of the pie mould together and stand on a baking tray. Put the large piece of pastry into the mould and work it up the sides with your fingers to $\frac{1}{4}$ inch above the top. Now put half the pork into the bottom of the pie, then the hard-boiled eggs, laying lengthways down the pie, and then cover with the grouse. Finally add the rest of the pork.

Form the remaining pastry into an oval, large enough to fit the top of the pie. Damp the edges of the pastry above the mould, place the lid in position, and press well into the pastry beneath. Trim the edges and set the trimmings aside in a warm place, for use as decoration. Crimp the pie edges and brush the surface with beaten egg. Make a large hole in the centre of the pie to allow steam to escape. Roll out the pastry scraps, cut diamond shapes for leaves and lay them round the hole. Cut a strip about 1 inch wide, fringe it along one edge with cuts about $\frac{1}{4}$ inch apart and roll it up to form a tassel. Place it carefully around the centre of the hole, but be careful not to block it. Brush this decoration with beaten egg.

Pre-heat your oven to 400° F (Gas 6) and place the pie in the centre of the oven. Bake for 30 minutes then reduce the heat to 350° F (Gas 4) for a further half hour. Now cover the pie with grease-proof paper and reduce the heat to 325° F (Gas 3) for a further hour. When the pie is cooked, take it from the oven, but leave it on the tray inside the mould until the following day.

Next day, heat the pie very slightly in order to loosen the mould, unclip it and remove. Melt the jellied stock from the grouse, cool it but do not allow it to set again. Now insert the

tip of a funnel into the hole in the pie centre, and carefully pour
in the liquid stock to fill the pie. Leave to cool so that the jelly
sets. When the pie is thoroughly cold, serve it with salad.

POTTED GROUSE

1 bird (or more)	clarified butter
butter or stock	salt and pepper
cayenne	

Roast the grouse if young, or casserole if old. Cool, then remove
the skin and bones from the bird, and mince or chop the meat
very finely. Pound the meat until it is quite smooth, and gradually add game stock or melted butter, until the mixture is soft
and moist. Season well with salt and pepper and a dash of
cayenne, and press the mixture into small pots. Cover with
clarified butter and use as required as a spread on biscuits or
bread or in pastry cases.

PARTRIDGE

In season 1 September to 1 February
The best bird for the table is considered to be the grey partridge,
and you can distinguish a young bird from an old one by the
fact that its long wing feather is pointed. In older birds this wing
feather is rounded. Its beak will be yellow and its legs dark.
Older birds must be braised, casseroled or marinated, even if
they have been hung for a number of days. Partridges should
be plucked, singed, cleaned and trussed as for pheasant.

ROAST PARTRIDGE

1 young partridge per person   1 slice bread per bird
1 rasher fat bacon per bird   salt and pepper
butter

Put a large piece of butter into the cavity of each prepared bird.
Season well, and then tie a rasher of fat bacon over each breast.
Place the birds in a baking tin in hot butter and roast them in
a medium-to-hot oven for about 20 minutes. 5 minutes before
the cooking time is up, remove the bacon so that the breasts
brown.

Meanwhile, fry the slices of bread in butter, removing the
crusts, and shaping the bread to make a cushion to receive the
partridges. Place each partridge on one of the croûtons, then
pour over them the butter and other juices from the roasting
pan. Serve with bread sauce, and fried or oven-baked bread-
crumbs and garnish with watercress.

PARTRIDGES IN VINE LEAVES

A well-known way of cooking partridges of any age is wrapped
in vine leaves. These can be obtained in tins or in brine from
many specialist delicatessen shops.

1 partridge per person   vine leaves
flour   salt and pepper
butter

Season the prepared partridges and place them in the butter
melted in a pan. Brown the birds all over, then remove them
from the pan and wrap each one in large vine leaves. Tie round
with fine string to hold in place. Now put the birds in a casserole,
pour over the melted butter, sprinkle with flour, add a little
more seasoning, then cover closely and cook in a moderate
oven, 350° F (Gas 4), for about an hour or until the birds are
tender, which will depend on their age.

VINE LEAF WRAPPED PARTRIDGES IN WINE

1 partridge per person	wine
vine leaves	salt and pepper
stock	

Wrap each seasoned partridge in vine leaves and place the birds in a casserole. Almost cover with a mixture half wine, half stock, and simmer for 35 minutes. Lift the birds from the casserole, place in a baking tin, baste with melted butter and roast for a further 25 minutes. Remove the vine leaves toward the end of the cooking, say for the last 5 minutes or so, to allow the breasts to brown. Make a gravy from the pan juices and the stock, and pour over the birds when serving with new potatoes and watercress.

FRENCH PARTRIDGES ON THE SPIT

1 partridge per person	1 slice bacon per bird
black olives	1 slice fried bread per bird
shelled walnuts	salt and pepper

Season the cavities of the prepared birds, from which the feet have been removed, with salt and pepper. Place two or three black olives inside, together with a few broken pieces of walnut. Wrap the birds in bacon, tie them with fine string, and skewer them on to a long spit, roasting over a good bed of glowing coals, and turning often. The birds can be cooked on a rotating electric spit. When the birds are cooked, remove the wrappings and serve on a slice of bread previously fried in butter.

STEWED PARTRIDGE

2 partridges	¼ pint port wine
1 oz butter	¼ pint white stock
2 tablespoons flour	salt and pepper

Dredge the birds inside and out with the seasonings. Melt the butter in a shallow pan, and in it fry the birds, turning occasionally, until they are evenly brown. Lift the birds on to a plate and add the flour to the butter in the pan, stirring until it becomes pale gold in colour. Now add the stock and wine, and when it is smooth and has reached boiling point, return the birds to the pan and cover closely. Simmer gently for about 1¾ hours. Serve garnished with watercress and accompanied by the gravy from the sauce-boat. Quite elderly birds will make a very nice meal when cooked in this manner.

FRIED PARTRIDGES

2 partridges	1 tablespoon chopped parsley
½ pint olive oil	browned bread-crumbs
1 bay leaf	salt and pepper

Using young partridges, cut them in two lengthwise, and flatten with a rolling pin. Make a marinade of the oil, salt, pepper, parsley and the bay leaf, dried and crushed. Place the pieces of bird in this marinade for an hour or longer if possible. Then lift the pieces from the oil, drain slightly, and then rub each in the browned bread-crumbs. Fry each piece on both sides in hot oil until the flesh is tender. As each portion of bird is ready, keep it warm on a serving dish until the rest of the cooking has been completed.

PARTRIDGE WITH CABBAGE

2 partridges	bouquet garni
1 medium cabbage	1 pint stock
4 oz bacon	nutmeg
1 onion	sausages (optional)
lard or margarine	salt and pepper

This is another recipe suitable for birds past their first youth. Cut the cabbage in quarters. Take off the outer leaves and the hardest part of the stalk, wash well and cook in boiling salted water for a few minutes. Drain well. Split the partridges in half and fry in the fat until golden brown and crisp. Line the casserole with the bacon slices, then put on top half the cabbage, season with salt and pepper, sprinkle with a little nutmeg, then put in the onion, thinly sliced, and on top of this the pieces of fried partridge. Now add the rest of the cabbage together with a little more seasoning, then almost cover with stock. Place the casserole lid in position and cook in the middle of the oven for about 1½ to 2 hours, adding a little more stock if necessary. Three or four chipolata sausages or 2 smoked sausages may if required be added to the casserole, or, if preferred, may be fried separately, and used as a garnish to the finished dish. Serve the pieces of bird on a bed of shredded cabbage. This quantity is sufficient for 4 servings.

PIGEON

Pigeons are available all the year round, but it is important, especially for roast pigeon, that the birds should be young, with pinkish legs and claws, well-covered limbs and breasts and skin which is not dark in colour. Young birds are, of course, smaller in size and their beaks look disproportionately large. They will not have grown the white neck ring. In an older bird the feet and legs are of a bright coral colour.

Pigeon is easy to pluck because the feathers are loose and the skin tough. Plucking, drawing and trussing are done in the same way as for other birds. Leave the feet on because it makes for simplicity in trussing and tying the legs together. Pigeon is liable to be dry, so that more fat bacon than usual should be used when roasting. Pigeon does not need hanging for more than a couple of days after shooting. Keep them in a cool, airy place, protected, of course, from flies.

Older birds, when cooked whole, have a tendency to impart a slightly bitter flavour to a dish. This derives from the back-bone, and it is therefore advisable when cooking a bird which has passed its youth to halve it and remove this back-bone.

ROAST PIGEON

2 young pigeons	2 slices fried bread or toast
2 oz butter	a little lemon juice
2 rashers fat bacon	salt and pepper

Mix the butter with the lemon juice and put half in each bird cavity, the birds having of course been previously prepared for roasting. Truss, cover each with fat bacon, tied in place, and roast in a fairly hot oven, 375° to 400° F (Gas 5–6), for about 30 minutes. Baste once or twice during this cooking time. Just before the bird is cooked, remove the bacon and allow it to brown for about 10 minutes. You can, if you wish, put the fried bread or toast under the birds at this stage for the final 10 minutes of cooking. Otherwise place the birds on the bread when the cooking is complete. Garnish with watercress and serve with gravy and bread sauce.

PIGEONS WITH GREEN PEAS

2 young pigeons	2 tablespoons whole berry
4 tablespoons corn oil	cranberry sauce
8 to 10 small white onions,	½ pint chicken stock
peeled	½ lb fresh green peas
4 oz bacon diced	bouquet garni
1 tablespoon cornflour	salt and pepper

Clean and truss as for roasting. Heat the corn oil in a casserole and sauté the pigeons until evenly browned. Remove the pigeons, add the onions and bacon and sauté until golden. Add the cornflour, stir in the chicken stock and cranberry sauce. Bring to the boil, stirring all the time. Add the pigeons, green peas and bouquet garni. Season to taste, cover and cook in a slow oven, 300° F (Gas 2) for 1¼ to 1½ hours.

CASSEROLED PIGEON

2 young pigeons	1 medium onion, chopped
3 oz bacon	1 oz butter

¾ pint stock	bouquet garni
1 carrot	salt and pepper
1 oz flour	

Prepare and truss the pigeons as for roasting. Melt the butter in a pan and in it fry the pigeons, bacon and onion until all are well browned. Transfer to a casserole, pour over the stock, add the bouquet garni and the vegetables, diced, cover and simmer until the birds are tender, about 1 to 1½ hours. Blend the flour into a little cold stock or water and add this to the casserole. Bring back to boiling point, stir, re-cover and simmer for a further 10 minutes. When the birds are cooked, lift from the casserole, cut off the trussing strings and split the birds in half. Place them on a hot serving-dish. Skim excess fat from the sauce and pour over the pieces of bird.

PIGEONS IN BEER

2 pigeons	flour
1 medium onion, sliced	olive oil
2 bay leaves	1 beaten egg yolk
beer (mild or bitter)	salt and pepper

Soak the pigeons' livers overnight in a marinade of beer, sliced raw onion, salt, pepper and bay leaves. Next day remove the livers from the marinade, dry, flour and fry them in a little olive oil. Split the birds in half, remove the back-bone and place the pieces together with the livers into a casserole. Pour over the marinade and add further beer (or, if you prefer, water) to cover the flesh. Simmer in the oven for about 1 to 1¼ hours until the meat lifts away from the bone without difficulty. Place the pieces of bird on a warm serving dish, strain the gravy into a small saucepan and stir in a beaten egg yolk to thicken, first of course removing the saucepan from the heat. Pour this sauce over the birds before serving.

PIGEON PUDDING

2 pigeons	2 hard-boiled eggs
6 oz rump steak	½ cup stock
1 tablespoon flour	salt and pepper

For the pastry

10 oz flour	level teaspoon baking powder
5 oz suet	pinch mixed herbs
pinch salt	cold water

If using butcher's suet chop it finely with flour. Make suet pastry, by sifting the flour, salt and baking powder together, and mixing in the suet and herbs. Add sufficient cold water to make a firm dough. Roll out the pastry, reserving a piece for the pudding lid and using the rest to line a basin. Remove the feet from the pigeons, then split the birds in half and remove the skin. Cut the steak into small cubes and dip both pigeon pieces and steak into seasoned flour. Cut the hard-boiled eggs into quarters. Into a lined basin put the prepared birds, steak and egg. Add the stock, cover with a lid made from the remaining pastry, and steam for 3 to 3½ hours. Meanwhile make some extra stock or gravy to serve with the pudding when ready.

GRILLED PIGEON

2 pigeons	salt and pepper
2 oz butter	slices of toast

Split the prepared birds down the back, flatten and cut away the back-bone. Brush the pieces all over with melted butter or cooking oil, season with salt and pepper and place under a pre-heated grill. Cook for about 20 minutes, turning occasionally. Serve on slices of toast or fried bread, and pour over the drippings from the grill pan.

PIGEON PIE

2 pigeons	1 dessertspoon flour
2 oz butter	¾ pint stock
8 oz bacon	½ teaspoon meat extract
1 onion	salt and pepper
2 tomatoes	

For the pastry

8 oz plain flour	3 oz lard
1 teaspoon baking powder	$\frac{1}{2}$ oz margarine
pinch of salt	cold water

Cook the pigeons in advance, before you want to use the pie at a meal. Heat the butter in a pan and in it fry the pigeons, halved lengthways and with back-bones removed, until they are well browned. Lift from the fat and place the pieces in a deep casserole. In the remaining fat fry the bacon until lightly brown, then sprinkle the bacon over the pigeons.

Fry the onion until brown and leave in the pan. Add the tomatoes, cook a further 5 minutes then sprinkle in the flour and stir over the heat, cooking for a further minute or two. Now add the stock, bring to the boil, stirring continuously, and boil for 3 minutes. Add the meat extract, seasoning and pour over the pigeons. Cover the casserole and cook in the middle of a moderate oven, pre-heated at 350° F (Gas 4) for about 1$\frac{1}{2}$ hours. Leave to cool.

Next day (or later the same day) make the pastry, by sifting together the salt and flour, rubbing in the fat, adding the baking powder, and mixing with a knife to a stiff dough with cold water. Roll out the pastry, brush the rim of the casserole with water and cut a strip of pastry to fit. Pile the pieces of pigeon up to the centre of the dish, moisten the pastry rim with water lightly, and then put in place the pastry lid, pressing firmly with the thumb all round the rim. Make a hole in the centre for the steam to escape. Trim with a few diamond-shaped leaves, made from rolled-out scraps of pastry, and brush round the hole at the top and place the leaves in position. Brush the top of the pie with milk or beaten egg, and bake in a pre-heated oven 400° F (Gas 6) on the second shelf from the top for about 30 to 35 minutes.

PIGEONS ITALIAN STYLE

2 pigeons	$\frac{1}{2}$ onion
2 oz butter	2 oz bacon
3 tablespoons oil	$\frac{1}{2}$ cup wine

a little rosemary and sage   1 (8 oz) tin tomatoes
1 small red pepper   salt and pepper

Cut the prepared pigeons into serving pieces, removing back-
bone. Heat the butter and oil together in a large, stout pan, and
in this brown the pigeon pieces, the onion and bacon. (The
onion should be thinly sliced.) Then add the wine and herbs,
the pepper, seeded and chopped, and salt and pepper to taste.
Cook until the wine has evaporated, then add the tomatoes,
and continue to cook over a moderate heat for a further 20 to
25 minutes, or until the pigeon pieces are quite tender.

SNIPE

In season 12 August to 31 January
Snipe can be eaten hung or unhung, according to personal taste.
The birds should be plucked, but not drawn. Pluck not only the
body but the head. Leave the head in position, but take the skin
off and remove the eyes. Wipe each bird, twist the head round
and, using the beak as a skewer, pass it through the legs and
into the body.

    Allow one bird per person as a general rule, or half a bird
each, depending on size. Brush each bird over with warmed
butter, then tie a thin slice of bacon over each breast and place
on a slice of toast in a baking tin. Cook in a moderate oven,
350° F (Gas 4), for 15 to 20 minutes, basting frequently with
the melted butter. The drippings from the trail will be caught
up into the toast. Dish the birds on this toast, garnish and serve
with gravy in a separate sauce-boat. Serve with fried bread-
crumbs and game chips, or a salad if preferred.

WOODCOCK

In season 1 September to 31 January (Scotland) and 1 October to 31 January (England)
Woodcock tends to be a little rubbery if eaten too fresh. It is therefore advisable to hang it for a day or two. Prepare and cook in exactly the same way as for Snipe above.

PLOVER

In season 1 September to 31 January
Only two kinds of plover are allowed to be shot in Britain – the Golden Plover and the Grey Plover. Other varieties are protected by the Protection of Birds Act (1954).

Prepare the birds and cook them as for snipe and woodcock on page 212 and above.

INDEX

Note: The asterisks indicate those recipes which are marked in the text with the economy symbol.

If you have enjoyed this PAN
Book, you may like to choose
your next book from the titles
listed on the following pages.

Marika Hanbury Tenison

DEEP-FREEZE COOKERY   45p

Truly comprehensive, it happily combines the general subject of deep-freezing with a host of delicious recipes all home-tried and tested.

Now that the deep-freeze is steadily gaining priority over the washing machine and spin dryer, this remarkable book should prove to be an invaluable guide for those who enjoy cooking yet do not want to waste long hours in the kitchen.

Advice includes:
Clear instructions on maintenance
What not to freeze
How to use the freezer as a budget saver
Practical charts and reference tables
Seasonal menus for special occasions

'Valuable advice . . . excellent help . . . what more could a deep-freeze owner want?'
                 — IDEAL HOME

Constance Spry
Rosemary Hume

THE CONSTANCE SPRY COOKERY
  BOOK (illus) £1.25

'Cooking is a combination of science, art, in-
vention, and a few other things' – Constance
Spry and Rosemary Hume, founders of the
Cordon Bleu Cookery School, share the secrets
of a lifetime of experience, covering all aspects
of cooking and entertaining, to make life easier
both for the novice cook and normally compe-
tent hostess in a tight spot. An imaginative
mine of information and inspiration for the
bored housewife. A must for every home.

'This fat, full, delectable opus could easily
prove the favourite wedding present. The
range is extraordinary. The book is admirably
bound and printed, and contains good photo-
graphs' – THE SUNDAY TIMES

Kenneth Lo

QUICK AND EASY CHINESE
COOKING   40p

At last – over two hundred authentic Chinese recipes that are not only quick and easy, but also can be made from ingredients you can buy in any foodstore or supermarket.

From snacks to dinner parties, for two people or ten, these delicious recipes are capable of infinite variety.

With this book, Kenneth Lo dispels the mystique of Chinese cooking, and with step by step instructions, makes it easy for you and your friends to enjoy a cuisine that is varied, nutritious, and extremely tasty.

'Wide-ranging recipes set out with clarity'
                    – BETTER HOMES AND GARDENS